Antitrust Developments in Europe 2001

Antitrust Developments in Europe 2001

Edited by
Romano Subiotto
and
Robbert Snelders

KLUWER LAW INTERNATIONAL
THE HAGUE / LONDON / NEW YORK

Published by:
Kluwer Law International
P.O. Box 85889, 2508 CN The Hague, The Netherlands
sales@kli.wkap.nl
http://www.kluwerlaw.com

Sold and Distributed in North, Central and South America by:
Kluwer Law International
101 Philip Drive, Norwell, MA 02061, USA
kluwerlaw@wkap.com

Sold and Distributed in all other countries by:
Kluwer Law International
Distribution Centre, P.O. Box 322, 3300 AH Dordrecht, The Netherlands

A CIP Catalogue record for this book is available from the Library of Congress

Printed on acid-free paper.

Typeset by *Steve Lambley Information Design*, The Hague.

ISBN 90-411-1901-9
© 2002 Kluwer Law International

Kluwer Law International incorporates the imprint of Martinus Nijhoff Publishers

This publication is protected by international copyright law.
All rights reserved. No part of this publication may be reproduced, stored in a retrieval system, or transmitted in any form or by any means, electronic, mechanical, photocopying, recording or otherwise, without the prior permission of the publishers.

TABLE OF CONTENTS

Foreword xiii

Part I: EC Competition Developments 1

1. Vertical Restraints 3
1.1. ECJ – Judgment 3
    Case C-453/99 Courage v Crehan 3
1.2. Commission – Decisions 5
    Glaxo Wellcome Dual Pricing System 5
    Michelin 6

2. Abuse of Market Power 10
2.1. ECJ – Judgments 10
    Case C-163/99 Portugal v Commission 10
    Case C-340/99 TNT Traco v Poste Italiane 11
    Case C-475/99 Ambulanz Glöckner v Landkreis Südwestpfalz 12
2.2. ECJ – Order 15
    Case C-497/99 Irish Sugar v Commission 15
2.3. Commission – Decisions 16
    Deutsche Post 16
    Duales System Deutschland AG 18
    IMS HEALTH 20
    Deutsche Post 21
    La Poste France 22
2.4. Commission – Guidelines 23
    Draft Guidelines on Market Analysis and the Calculation of
    Significant Market Power for Electronic Communications
    Networks and Services 23

Table of Contents

3. Mergers and Acquisitions 26
    3.1. Notice 26
        Notice on Remedies 26
    3.2. Prohibition Decisions 29
        Metsä Tissue/SCA Mölnlycke 29
        General Electric/Honeywell 31
        Schneider Electric/Legrand 33
        Tetra Pak/Sidel 34
    3.3. Second-Phase Decisions with Undertakings 36
        EDF/EnBW 36
        ADtranz/Bombardier 38
        Hidroelectrica del Cantabrico/Villar Mir/EnBW 39
        Hutchinson/RMPM/ECT 40
    3.4. Second-Phase Decisions without Undertakings 41
        MAN/Auwärter 41
        BASF/Eurodiol/Pantochim 42
        UPM-Kymmene/Norske Skog/Haindl 43
    3.5. First-Phase Decisions with Undertakings 44
        United Airlines/US Air 44
        Degussa/Laporte 46
        Seagram/Pernod Ricard/Diageo 46
        Nestlé/Ralston Purina 47
    3.6. First-Phase Decision without Undertakings 48
        Philips/Marconi Medical Systems 48

4. Joint Ventures 49
        Smith & Nephew/Beiersdorf 49
        The Post Office/TNT/Singapore Post 49
        T-Online/TUI/C&N 50
        IBM Italia/Business Solutions 51
        Covisint 52
        Hutchinson/NTT DoCoMo/KPN Mobile 52
        Hitachi/LG Electronics 53
        BP Chemicals/Solvay 54

5. State Aid 55

5.1. ECJ – Judgments 55
    Case C-99/98 Austria v Commission 55
    Case C-379/98 PreussenElektra v Schlesswag 56
    Case C-204/97 Portuguese Republic v Commission 58
    Case C-143/99 Adria-Wien Pipeline v Finanzlandesdirektion für Kärnten 58
    Case C-53/00 Ferring v Agence Centrale des Organismes de
    Sécurité Sociale 60
5.2. CFI – Judgments 62
    Case T-156/98 RJB Mining v Commission 62
    Case T-288/97 Regione Autonoma Friuli-Venezia Giulia v Commission 63

6. Policy and Procedure 65

6.1. CFI – Judgments 65
    Case T-112/98 Mannesmannröhren-Werke AG v Commission 65
    Cases T-202/98, T-204/98 and T-207/98 Tate & Lyle,
    British Sugar and Napier Brown v Commission 66
    Case T-112/99 Métropole Télévision (M6), Suez-Lyonnaise des Eaux,
    France Télécom and Télévision Française 1 SA (TF1) v Commission 68
    Case T-171/99 Corus UK Ltd. v Commission 69
    Cases T-45/98 and T-47/98 Krupp Thyssen Stainless GmbH and Acciai
    Speciali Terni SpA v Commission 71
6.2. Commission – Decision 72
    Amino Acids 72
6.3. Commission – Notices 74
    Draft Leniency Notice 74
    General Application of the Leniency Notice 75
    De Minimis Notice 75

Part II: National Competition Developments 77

1. Austria 79

1.1. Abuse of Market Power 79
    Austrian Postal Operator 79
    Non-Cash Payment Systems 80

Table of Contents

1.2. Mergers and Acquisitions 80
    Format/profil 80
    Linde-Verlag/Wolters Kluwer 81
1.3. Joint Ventures 82
    Cooperative and Concentrative Joint Ventures 82

2. Belgium 84

2.1. Abuse of Market Power 84
    BVBA Incine/NV Rendac 84
2.2. Mergers and Acquisitions 85
    Vinci/Groupe GTM 85
    De Beers/Rio Tinto/Ashton Mining; P&O/Antwerp Combined
    Terminals 85
2.3. Policy and Procedure 86
    "New Hearing" Rule in Merger Proceedings 86
    Removal of Members of the Competition Service 87
    Council Annual Report 87
    Intervention of the Competition Council before the Court of Appeals 87
    New Merger Notification Thresholds 87

3. Denmark 89

3.1. Vertical Restraints 89
    Tryg Baltica 89
    Den Almindelige Danske Lægeforening 89
    Carlsberg 90
    Danish Football Association 90
    Real Estate Franchise Chain 90
3.2. Abuse of Market Power 91
    Dansk Kørelærer Union 91
    Opel Danmark 91
    Ruko 92
3.3. Mergers and Acquisitions 92
    DONG/Naturgas Sjælland 92
    AB/Provinzial 93
    Højgaard & Schultz/Monberg & Thorsen 94
    Carlsberg/Coca-Cola Bottlers 94

3.4. Policy and Procedure 94
   Agreement between Nordic Competition Authorities 94
   Nordic Competition Meeting 94
   Proposed Amendments to Competition Act 95

4. France 97

4.1. Vertical Restraints 97
   Canal+ 97
   Benetton 99
4.2. Horizontal Agreements 100
   Banking Sector Cartel 100
   Accor/Sodhexo/Chèque-Déjeuner 101
   Concrete Industry Cartel 101
   Construction Industry Cartel 101
4.3. Abuse of Market Power 102
   France Télécom 102
4.4. Mergers and Acquisitions 102
   Boeing/Jeppesen Group 102
4.5. Policy and Procedure 103
   Amendments to Competition Law 103

5. Germany 104

5.1. Horizontal Agreements 104
   Ready-Mixed Concrete Industry Cartel 104
   Inter-bank Charge for Eurocheque Card Payments 104
5.2. Abuse of Market Power 105
   Electricity Sector Proceedings 105
5.3. Mergers and Acquisitions 105
   Goodyear/Michelin 105
   Kirch Group/EM.TV 105
   Callahan Associates/NetCologne 106
   Lekkerland/Tobaccoland 106
   VEBA/VIAG; RWE/VEW 107
   Deutsche Lufthansa/Eurowings 107
   Sanacorp/Andreae-Noris Zahn 108
   Deutsche Post/trans-o-flex Schnell-Lieferdienst 108
   BP/Veba Oel; Shell/DEA 109
   Promatech/Sulzer 109

Table of Contents

5.4. Policy and Procedure 110
    Electricity Sector Decision Body 110

6. Greece 112

6.1. Vertical Restraints 112
    Communication on Vertical Agreements 112
6.2. Abuse of Market Power 113
    GlaxoWellcome 113

7. Italy 115

7.1. Horizontal Agreements 115
    Otis/Ceam/Kone/Schindler 115
    Telecom Italia Mobile/Omnitel Pronto Italia 116
    Unione Petrolifera 116
7.2. Abuse of Market Power 117
    Telecom Italia 117
    Alitalia (I) 118
    Alitalia (II) 119
7.3. Mergers and Acquisitions 119
    Seat Pagine Gialle/Cecchi Gori Communications 119
    Granarolo/Centrale del Latte di Vicenza 120
    Enel/France Télécom/Infostrada 121
    Promatech/Sulzer 122
7.4. Policy and Procedure 122
    Amendments to Competition Law 122
    New Merger Notification Thresholds 123

8. The Netherlands 124

8.1. Policy and Procedure 124
    Change in Competition Authority Status 124
    Competition Authority 2000 Annual Report 125
    New Merger Notification Thresholds 125
    Fining Guidelines 126

9. Spain 127

9.1. Vertical Restraints 127
    La Casera 127

9.2. Horizontal Agreements 127
    Madrid Airport Cargo Operators 127
    Dairy Cartel 128
9.3. Abuse of Market Power 129
    Telefónica Móviles 129
    Cepsa/Repsol 129
    Empresa Mixta de Servicios Funerarios de Madrid 130
9.4. Mergers and Acquisitions 130
    Endesa/Iberdrola 130
    Pio Coronado/Cemetro 131
    Nutreco España/Agrovic Alimentación 131
    Iberdrola Redes 132
    Promatech/Sulzer 132
9.5. Joint Ventures 133
    Terra Networks/Banco Bilbao Vizcaya Argentaria 133
9.6. Policy and Procedure 133
    Draft Regulation on Agreements Qualifying for EC Block Exemptions .. 133
    Draft Law regarding Regional Competition Authorities 134
    OECD Recommendation on Tribunal 134
    Amendments to Competition Law 135
    Decree on Merger Control Procedure 135

10. Sweden **138**
10.1. Horizontal Agreements 138
    Uponor/Aktiebolaget Svenska Wavin/KWH PIPE Sverige 138
10.2. Abuse of Market Power 138
    Scandinavian Airline System 138
10.3. Mergers and Acquisitions 139
    Svenska Girot/Bankgirocentralen BGC/Privatgirot/Postgirot 139
10.4. Policy and Procedure 140
    Group Exemption Regulations 140

11. Switzerland **141**
11.1. Horizontal Agreements 141
    Swiss Association of Booksellers/Börsenverein des Deutschen
    Buchhandels 141
    Betosan/Isotech/Renersco/Weiss et Appetito 141

xi

Table of Contents

11.2. Abuse of Market Power 142
    Teleclub 142
    Swisscom 142
11.3. Mergers and Acquisitions 143
    Banque Nationale de Paris/Paribas 143
    Le Monde/Le Temps 143
11.4. Policy and Procedure 143
    FCC Annual Report 143
    Proposed Amendments to Competition Act 143
    Foreign Concentrations 144
    Draft Act on Radio and Television 144
    Life Insurance Market Recommendation 144

12. The United Kingdom 146

12.1. Vertical Restraints 146
    Termination of Medications Retail Price Maintenance Exemption 146
12.2. Abuse of Market Power 147
    Napp Pharmaceuticals 147
    Banking Sector Complex Monopoly 147
    Yellow Pages 149
    British Sky Broadcasting Limited 149
    Dixons 150
    Consignia 150
    General Insurance Standards Council 150
    Aberdeen Journals 151
    ICL 152
    Mobile Phone Sector Inquiry 153
12.3. Mergers and Acquisitions 154
    Interbrew 154
    Lloyds TSB/Abbey National 156
    Govia/Connex 157
    Promatech/Sulzer 158
    Cargill/Cerestar 158
12.4. Policy and Procedure 158
    Transport Ticket Block Exemption 158
    Competition Regime Reforms 158
    Proposed Criminalization of "Hard Core" Cartel Activities 159
    Competition in Professions Report 160

Table of Cases 163
Keyword Index 169

FOREWORD

Cleary, Gottlieb, Steen & Hamilton has a long-standing commitment to the practice of law in Europe. The firm's advisory work for the French Government, and in particular Jean Monnet, on the implementation of the Marshall Plan led to the opening of the firm's first European office in Paris in 1949. In the following years, the firm was invited to assist in the drafting of certain provisions of the Treaties of the European Communities, including its antitrust rules, and to advise and represent the European Commission and the European Atomic Energy Agency. The opening of the Brussels office in 1960 was followed by the opening of offices in London in 1971, Frankfurt in 1991, Moscow in 1992, and Rome and Milan in 1998.

Cleary Gottlieb's antitrust practice is among the largest and longest-established in the world, comprising around 20 partners and over 80 associates based in Washington D.C., Brussels, Paris, Rome, Frankfurt, and London. The firm's European offices have developed a fully-integrated European antitrust law practice with extensive and varied expertise in advising plaintiffs, complainants, and defendants on the application of EC and national antitrust laws to domestic and cross-border mergers, acquisitions, joint ventures, and minority holdings; relations among competitors and among companies operating at different levels of trade; the behavior of dominant companies; the application of state aid rules; proceedings before the European Commission and national antitrust authorities; arbitration; and litigation before the European Courts and national courts.

Monitoring legal developments is an indispensable element in maintaining the ability to advise and represent clients at the highest level. Cleary Gottlieb has meticulously monitored and informed its clients of the most significant competition developments in Europe since the early 1970s. As an increasing number of EU Member States have adopted antitrust laws, the monitoring has extended to significant national developments in the most active Member States.

We felt that the time had come to share the results of this monitoring with a broader audience. It is Cleary Gottlieb's hope that readers will find the contents of this book helpful in learning about or advising on competition law in Europe. The book is divided into two main parts, Part I – EC Competition Developments and Part II – National Competition Developments. Part I is further broken down into topical sections related to Vertical Restraints, Abuse of Market Power, Mergers

Foreword

and Acquisitions, Joint Ventures, State Aid, and Policy and Procedure. Within these sections, we have added sub-headings to distinguish among the various types of proceedings relevant to that section (*e.g.*, State Aid – CFI – Judgments, or Mergers and Acquisitions – Second Phase Decisions with Undertakings). Part II is first broken down by jurisdiction, and then by topical headings similar to those used in Part I (*e.g.*, France – Vertical Restraints).

Of course, one single person cannot monitor all developments. As with most achievements, the contents of this book are the result of teamwork. We thank all the Cleary Gottlieb partners, counsel and associates who have contributed to this work, including Stephan Barthelmess, François Brunet, Maurits Dolmans, David Gelfand, Wolfgang Knapp, Nicholas Levy, Mario Siragusa, Dirk Vandermeersch, Antoine Winckler, Asger Petersen, John Temple Lang, Claudia Annacker, Matteo Beretta, Gaëlle Bontinck, Christopher Cook, Rupert Elderkin, Christoph Feddersen, Thomas Graf, Ianis Girgenson, Jacob Grierson, Silke Heinz, Daniel Ilan, Paul Laikin, Cynthia Ngwe, Johanne Peyre, Neil Rigby, Robert Shulz, Igor Simic, Sergio Sorinas, Despina Spanou, David Stiepleman, Saverio Valentino, Olivier Van Obberghen, David Went and Peter Werdmuller. Additionally, we are grateful to a number of Cleary Gottlieb alumni and other lawyers who have made contributions to our monitoring efforts, including Steven Allcock, Alejandro Fernandez de Araoz, Christer Danielsson, Beatriz Delgado Clemente, Edoardo Gambaro, Jörg Häring, Elizabeth Harwick, Christian Lundgren, Blanca Montejo, Irene Tencate, Silvio Venturi and Andrew Ward. We also wish to thank the members of our Brussels office legal support team who have provided research and administrative assistance on this publication, including Paola Cedrangolo, Kathleen Martens, Els Merchiers, Ann Moens, Katrien Verfaillie and Kerri Vermeylen. Finally, we extend a special thank you to Cleary Gottlieb lawyer Charles Berger for helping to oversee this project.

Romano Subiotto and Robbert Snelders
Brussels, June 2002

PART I: EC COMPETITION DEVELOPMENTS

1. VERTICAL RESTRAINTS

1.1. ECJ – JUDGMENT

Case C-453/99 Courage v Crehan

This case concerned a dispute between Courage Ltd. and Crehan, a tenant of a beer establishment. The parties had entered into two 20-year leases requiring Crehan to purchase beer exclusively from Courage. In 1993, Courage brought an action against Crehan for unpaid deliveries. Crehan objected that the exclusive purchase obligation contained in the lease was contrary to Article 81(1) EC and counter-claimed for damages.

On March 22, Advocate General Mischo rendered his opinion, focusing on whether a party to an agreement contrary to Article 81(1) may invoke this provision to claim damages, and whether the answer should differ if the applicable national law prohibits a party to an illegal agreement from claiming damages from the other party.

The Advocate General, citing the *BTR* and *Delimitis* judgments,[1] recalled that a party to a prohibited agreement may rely on the nullity of the agreement before the courts. The Advocate General added that Article 81(1) protects not only third parties from the effect of an illegal agreement, but also, in exceptional circumstances, a party to the agreement where that party bears no significant responsibility for the distortion of competition, *e.g.*, a party in a weak bargaining position in the context of a vertical relationship practically required to accept restrictive terms. National courts are also obliged to safeguard the rights created for individuals by Article 81(1).

The Advocate General concluded that EC law precludes a rule of national law preventing a party subject to an infringing contract from recovering damages simply because it is a party to that contract. However, a party's failure to decline the agreement may limit the damages actually recoverable.

---

[1] Case 127/73 *BTR* 1974 ECR 51 and Case C-234/89 *Delimitis* 1991 ECR I-935.

On September 20, the Court of Justice followed the Advocate General's opinion in ruling that: (i) damages can be claimed before national courts for breaches of Article 81; and (ii) parties to agreements violating Article 81 cannot be barred from claiming damages against co-contractors before national courts.[2] In so doing, the Court overturned the principle of English law that a party to an illegal act may not benefit from its own wrongdoing, and therefore may not recover damages from other parties to an illegal agreement.

The Court reaffirmed that it is for national law to provide procedural rules, including remedies, for breaches of EC law, provided that: (i) the remedy must not be less favorable than that available for domestic claims; and (ii) the remedy must not render ineffective the right under EC law. A national court may act to prevent unjust enrichment to litigants, and may consequently prevent a party from benefiting from its own unlawful conduct by denying damages. However, damages may be denied only to parties that bear "significant responsibility" for the distortion of competition arising from an agreement (in contrast to the Advocate General's reference to "more than negligible" or "at least equal" responsibility).

In determining whether a party bears significant responsibility, the Court listed two main factors to be taken into account: (i) the economic and legal context; and (ii) the respective bargaining power of the parties, in particular whether the party seeking damages was in a "markedly weaker position" than the other party, so as to call into question seriously that party's freedom to negotiate the terms of the contract and capacity to avoid or reduce the losses suffered. Note that the Advocate General stated that a party is still required to take reasonable efforts to mitigate the loss, whereas the Court seems to require that the party show that it lacked the capacity to take action at all.

The Court also added to the Advocate General's opinion by stating that a contract might prove to be contrary to Article 81(1) for the sole reason that it is part of a network of similar contracts which have a cumulative detrimental effect on competition. In such case, the party contracting with the person controlling the network cannot bear significant responsibility for the breach of Article 81, particularly where in practice the terms of the contract were imposed by the party controlling the network. As a result, pub tenants and other members of large distribution networks may be regarded from the outset as not significantly responsible, and therefore entitled to bring claims for damages where the network is found contrary to Article 81.

---

[2] 2001 ECR I-6297.

1.2. COMMISSION – DECISIONS

Glaxo Wellcome Dual Pricing System

On May 8, the Commission prohibited a dual pricing system under which Glaxo Wellcome (GW) charged wholesalers in Spain higher prices for GW products they planned to export to other Member States, compared to the prices charged for GW products they planned to sell in Spain.[3] The prohibition itself does not come as a great surprise. More noteworthy is the Commission's detailed rejection of GW's arguments in defense of the dual pricing system.

GW admitted that its pricing system was designed to restrict parallel trade, but argued that it did not restrict competition. The different prices prevailing in the Member States, GW argued, did not result from the system, but from the varying national price regulations. Moreover, GW claimed that even if the pricing system did restrict competition, consumer welfare arguments justified the restriction.

The Commission followed the reasoning of the earlier judgment of the Court of Justice in *Merck v Primecrown*,[4] which applied the principle of the free movement of goods, notwithstanding the existence of divergent national regulations imposing sale prices and reimbursement levels, and extended this logic to the application of the competition provisions of the EC Treaty.

Contrary to GW's contention that price levels in Spain resulted from government intervention, the Commission found that GW had some influence in setting the prices and had been active in negotiating prices, including price increases. In addition, GW had admitted that parallel trade was legitimate if it arose from currency fluctuations rather than price regulations, yet the dual pricing system had the effect of severely limiting the possibility of parallel trade from Spain to other Member States for most of GW's products, thereby cutting off an alternative source of supply for the products and limiting price competition.

The Commission rejected GW's claim that the losses incurred as a result of parallel trade would undermine its research and development budget, which would in turn affect the development of new drugs. The Commission found that there was no causal link between such losses and the research and development investments made, that such losses would in any event be insignificant, and that the losses could be deducted from other items in the budget. GW also claimed that

---

[3] OJ 2001 L 302/1; Commission Press Release IP/01/661 May 8, 2001.
[4] Joined Cases C-267/95 and C-268/95 1996 ECR I-6285.

parallel trade exports from Spain would result in a shortage of supply on the Spanish market, a claim for which the Commission found no evidence.

By rejecting this attempt to justify a restriction of competition, the Commission indicated that the existence of government price intervention in pharmaceuticals does not justify altering its analysis of effect on competition, and that the objective of integrating national markets is of paramount importance in EC competition law.

Michelin

On June 20, the Commission imposed a fine of € 19.76 million on La Manufacture Française de Pneumatiques Michelin for abusing its dominant position in the French markets for new replacement tires for heavy vehicles and for retreaded tires for heavy vehicles by operating a complex system of quantitative rebates, bonuses and commercial agreements that induced the loyalty of its dealers.[5]

In *Hoffmann-La Roche*, the Court of Justice held that a dominant undertaking may not grant discounts conditional on the purchaser's obtaining all or most of its requirement from the dominant undertaking, because such discounts are granted not on the basis of cost savings to the supplier, but rather to prevent customers from obtaining their supplies from competing producers. Quantitative rebates linked exclusively to the volume of purchases were nevertheless allowed.[6] Later, in the first Michelin case, the Court prohibited increasing discounts on a customer's entire annual purchases of Michelin products depending on the customer's achieving turnover targets in Michelin products in that year (so-called "target rebates"). The Court noted that the rebates concerned were not based on any economically justifiable countervailing advantage.[7] It added that the discounts' binding effect was exacerbated by the duration of the reference periods and by the fact that the targets were not revealed to customers.

The Commission's decisional practice in this area is also of interest. In 1989, the Commission terminated proceedings under Article 82 EC against the Coca-Cola Export Corporation subject to Coca-Cola's agreeing, in particular, to refrain

---

[5] OJ 2002 L 143/1.

[6] Case 85/76 1979 ECR 461.

[7] Commission decision: Case IV/29.491 *Bandengroothandel Frieschebrug BV/NV Nederlandsche Banden-Industrie Michelin* OJ 1981 L 353/33. Judgment of the Court of Justice: Case 322/81 *Michelin v Commission* 1983 ECR 3461.

from granting target rebates relating to a reference period exceeding three consecutive months. The Commission accepted rebates relating to a three-month period where the targets were set by reference to the volumes purchased in the corresponding three-month period in the previous year.[8] The Commission applied the same principle in *Coca-Cola/Amalgamated Beverages*, when it cleared the acquisition only after Coca-Cola committed, in particular, to refrain from granting rebates relating to a reference period of more than three months.[9] Finally, in *British Airways/Virgin*, the Commission condemned British Airways (BA) for granting rebates to travel agents on all BA tickets they sold in a particular month upon achieving targets based on their ticket sales in the same month of the previous year. Relying on the Court's rulings in *Hoffmann-La Roche* and *Michelin*, the Commission stated that a dominant supplier can give discounts reflecting economies of scale benefiting the supplier, for example discounts for large orders that allow the supplier to produce large batches of product, but cannot give discounts or incentives to encourage loyalty. The Commission found that BA's schemes were not related to any economies of scale, but rather designed to encourage agents to sell BA tickets instead of tickets of competing carriers.[10]

In this case, the Commission interpreted the Court's case law to state that target rebates are abusive whenever the reference period exceeds "a reasonable period of three months," and that, contrary to Michelin's argument, the Court in the first Michelin case had not regarded the lack of transparency in rebates as an essential condition for the existence of an abuse. The Commission found that Michelin had abusively granted annual rebates on turnover achieved with Michelin France for tires. To be eligible, the dealer had to achieve pre-determined turnover targets. The rebates were not paid until February in the year following that in which the tire

---

[8] XIXth Report on Competition Policy, 1989, 65. The three-month reference period was based on an *obiter dictum* in a judgment of the German Cartel Court of November 12, 1980 (Kammergericht – Kart 32/79 *Fertigfutter*). In that case, the Court indicated that target rebates granted by dominant undertakings can be considered reasonable under German antitrust law – which reflects Article 82 EC – when they are based on reference periods of a few weeks or months. In practice, the German Cartel Office has agreed in a number of cases on target rebates based on a three-month reference period (*Deutsche Zündholzfabriken*, FCO Report 1983/84, p. 86, and *Dachentwässerungsartikel*, FCO Report 1984/85, p. 65).

[9] OJ 1997 L 218/15.

[10] OJ 2000 L 30/1.

Part I: EC Competition Developments

purchases were made. Given the intensity of competition and the low level of margins in the sector, dealers were obliged to resell at a loss pending the payment of the rebates. Since the rebates applied to the entire turnover achieved with Michelin and were calculated only about one year after the start of the first purchases, it was not possible for the dealers to determine the real unit purchase price of the tires before placing their last orders. This placed them in a situation of uncertainty and insecurity, prompting them to minimize their risks by purchasing mainly from Michelin. The annual reference period and the low profit margins increased the pressure on dealers to purchase from Michelin and to earn an additional rebate. Moreover, dealers were forced to agree on new quantitative commitments with Michelin before they had even received the quantity rebates for the previous year.

The Commission thus applied the Court's reasoning in *Michelin* to conclude that the system increased the pressure on the buyer to reach the purchase figure needed to obtain the discount, thereby avoiding a foreseeable loss for the entire period. In essence, a dealer could not take the risk at any given moment of diversifying its range to any significant extent at Michelin's expense, since this could have jeopardized its ability to reach the rebate threshold and could thus have had a major effect on the overall cost price of the Michelin tires purchased over the year.

The rebates also had a market partitioning effect because they applied only to purchases made from Michelin France and thus discouraged purchases made abroad or from importers. Conversely, the high level of prices in France, before rebates, discouraged purchases in France from abroad.

Michelin's abusive service bonus was an additional incentive proposed by Michelin to the specialized dealer to improve its equipment and after-sales service. The size of the bonus was fixed at the beginning of the year by agreement with the dealer, based on compliance with commitments entered into by the dealer in a number of areas. Each commitment corresponded to a number of points, and exceeding certain points thresholds triggered the bonus, which corresponded to a percentage of the turnover achieved with Michelin. The Commission concluded that the service bonus was unfair because it enabled Michelin to make a subjective assessment affecting the amount of the bonus. This allowed the manufacturer's representative to put strong pressure on the dealer as regards future commitments and, if necessary, to use the arrangement in a discriminatory manner. This bonus also had a tying effect, since one point was granted if the dealer committed itself to returning used Michelin tires systematically to Michelin for retreading.

Michelin's abusive progress bonus was intended to reward dealers who agreed at the beginning of the year to undertake in writing to exceed a minimum base, fixed by common agreement, depending on past performance and future prospects and who managed to exceed it. The base was proposed each year and was negotiated with the dealer. The minimum base corresponded either to the previous year's purchases or to the average of the last two or three years.

Michelin's abusive invoice bonus replaced the target rebate system in 1997. It was granted based on the number of new truck/earthmover/light plant tires purchased during the previous year, the average for the two previous years, or the average for the three previous years, depending on which was most favorable to the dealer. This appeared to be less unfair and less loyalty-inducing, since it automatically granted the dealer a rebate determined by previous performance. However, any additional purchase of Michelin products could enable the dealer to obtain a higher invoice rebate rate the following year, which had a loyalty-inducing effect.

Michelin's abusive target bonus was granted upon achievement of a specific net annual invoiced turnover target. The target was established based on the dealer's potential (its performance in previous years) and the anticipated trend on the market. Michelin gave the dealer the choice between its figures for the previous year and the average for the last two or three years. As in the case of the quantity rebates, this was found abusive because the rebates were based on the quantities sold during a relatively long reference period. The achieved-target bonus had an additional abusive effect, since the system gave the dealer a strong incentive to choose the highest of the three offered targets, making it difficult to reduce overall purchases from Michelin.

The Commission also found the agreements between Michelin and its dealers abusive. The first agreement, for optimum use of Michelin truck tires, required that Michelin casings be sent for retreading to Michelin exclusively, and granted a bonus for each casing sent. The second agreement (the so-called "Club" agreement) required dealers to promote the Michelin brand and not to divert spontaneous customer demand away from Michelin tires. It also allowed Michelin an exceptionally far-reaching right to monitor dealers' activities. The Commission stated that conduct on the part of an undertaking holding a dominant position which has the object or effect of binding dealers closely to it in organizational and commercial terms can only increase their dependence and is therefore abusive.

2. ABUSE OF MARKET POWER

2.1. ECJ – JUDGMENTS

Case C-163/99 Portugal v Commission

On March 29, the Court of Justice rejected an application for the annulment of a Commission decision relating to a system of rebates on landing fees in three Portuguese airports managed by a public undertaking.[11] The Commission had found that the system included two kinds of discounts that violated Article 82 EC in conjunction with Article 86(3) EC: a 50% discount for internal flights and an additional rebate granted to airlines performing a large number of landings in the relevant airports.

The Court stated that an undertaking occupying a dominant position is entitled to offer its customers quantity discounts linked solely to the volume of purchases made from it. However, the rules for calculating such discounts must not result in the application of dissimilar conditions to equivalent transactions with other trading parties within the meaning of subparagraph (c) of the second paragraph of Article 82 EC. Consequently, a system of quantity discounts violates Article 82 where, as a result of the thresholds of the various discount bands and the levels of discount offered, discounts (or additional discounts) are enjoyed by only some trading parties, giving them an economic advantage which is not justified by the volume of their business.

The Court considered that, absent any objective justification, setting a high threshold which can be met only by a few particularly large partners of the dominant undertaking, or a non-linear progression in the increase of the quantity discounts, may constitute evidence of discriminatory treatment.

In this case, the highest discount rate (32.7% at Lisbon Airport and 40.6% at other airports) was enjoyed only by the airlines TAP and Portugalia. In addition, the increase in the discount rate was appreciably greater for the highest band than for the lower bands (except for the lowest band for airports other than Lisbon

---

[11] 2001 ECR I-2613.

Airport). Absent any specific objective justification, the discount for the highest band was thus found to be excessive in comparison with the discounts for the lower bands.

Portugal submitted information relating to the advantage for airports of operating a system of quantity discounts on landing charges and argued that the system was open to all airlines. However, the Court considered such arguments to be insufficient in a situation where the system of discounts appears to favor certain airlines, in this case the national airlines, and where the airports concerned are likely to enjoy a natural monopoly for a very large portion of their activities.

Case C-340/99 TNT Traco v Poste Italiane

An Italian statute requiring firms that provide non-universal postal services (*e.g.*, express mail service) to pay Poste Italiane for universal postal services reserved to Poste Italiane (though such universal service was not provided to such firms) was found to violate Article 86(1) and Article 82 EC by the Court of Justice on May 17.[12]

The Court based its holding on the principle that a dominant undertaking abuses its dominance if it charges fees that are unfair or disproportionate to the economic value of the service provided or, *a fortiori*, if a fee is requested for services that the claimant undertaking has not itself supplied. The statute made this abuse inevitable.

According to the Court's case law, merely creating a dominant position by the grant of special or exclusive rights is not, in itself, incompatible with Article 86(1) in conjunction with Article 82. A Member State contravenes those provisions only if it: (i) endorses an abuse committed by the grantee of the exclusive rights;[13] (ii) enables the grantee to achieve goals that would have involved a violation of Article 82 if it had achieved them without state assistance;[14] or (iii) creates a situation in which the grantee either cannot avoid abusing its dominant position[15] or is led to abuse its dominant position.[16]

---

[12] 2001 ECR I-4109.

[13] See Case C-18/93 *Corsica Ferries* 1994 ECR I-1783.

[14] See Case C-18/88 *RTT* 1991 ECR I-5941.

[15] See Case C-41/90 *Höfner* 1991 ECR I-1979.

[16] See Case C-260/89 *ERT* 1991 ECR I-2925.

This last situation, in which an undertaking entrusted with exclusive rights is led to abuse its dominant position, could take place under two different sets of circumstances. First, a state measure could create a conflict of interest between two commercial activities of that undertaking, or between the undertakings' economic interests and a regulatory function entrusted to it. Second, the state could prohibit by statute the participation of other private undertakings in the market even though the monopoly holder is manifestly not in a position to satisfy prevailing market demand.

In both cases, it is not necessary to establish an actual abuse of a dominant position. A legal framework that is likely to create a situation where the undertaking is led to abuse its position must be regarded as being in itself contrary to Article 86(1) in conjunction with Article 82.

In this case, the Court also examined the applicability of the exception set forth in Article 86(2), which permits a Member State to grant special or exclusive rights to an undertaking entrusted with the operation of services of general economic interest so long as (i) the particular task assigned to that undertaking can be performed only through the grant of such rights, and (ii) the development of trade would not be affected in a way contrary to the interests of the Community.

Note that, for Article 86(2) to be applicable, it is not necessary that the financial balance or economic viability of the undertaking entrusted with the service of general economic interest be threatened. It is sufficient that, without the special rights, the undertaking could not perform the particular tasks entrusted to it.

The Court considered whether it would ever be necessary to require suppliers of non-universal postal services to finance universal service to enable Post Italiane to perform the tasks entrusted to it. The Court stressed that this would be the case only if (i) it could be shown that the proceeds were necessary to enable Poste Italiane to operate the universal postal service in economically acceptable conditions (*i.e.*, not exceeding what is necessary to offset losses incurred in providing the universal service); (ii) when providing a non-universal service, Poste Italiane pays the same dues for universal service as required from its competitors; and (iii) the non-universal services provided by the dominant operator are not subsidized by the universal services it operates.

Case C-475/99 Ambulanz Glöckner v Landkreis Südwestpfalz

This case involved a German requirement that private operators of ambulance services are to be refused authorization to provide independent ambulance services where the grant of such an authorization would be likely to affect adversely the operation or the profitability of the public ambulance service. The rule covered both emergency transport and patient transport (transport of ill or injured persons, or persons otherwise in need of help who are not emergency patients). At issue was the compatibility of the rule with Article 86 EC.

The matter came before Advocate General Jacobs, who rendered his opinion on May 17. The Advocate General first examined whether the public ambulance service is among the "undertakings to which Member States grant special or exclusive rights." The Advocate General considered the four essential elements of "special or exclusive rights" under Article 86(1): (i) they are granted by the authorities of a member state; (ii) they are granted to one undertaking or to a limited number of undertakings; (iii) they substantially affect the ability of other undertakings to exercise the economic activity in question in the same geographical area under substantially equivalent conditions; and (iv) they are granted otherwise than according to objective, proportional and non-discriminatory criteria.

Advocate General Jacobs found that the public ambulance service benefited from "special or exclusive rights" within the meaning of Article 86(1).

Nevertheless, because the granting of special or exclusive rights involves difficult economic assessments and social choices, Member States must enjoy a certain discretion in deciding whether a monopolist deserves such state protection. The court has therefore to limit its review to national provisions that are manifestly inappropriate.

Advocate General Jacobs mentioned several possible economic reasons for protecting the public ambulance service against competition from independent operators. The presence of independent operators on the market naturally reduces the revenue of the public ambulance service. It is also to be expected that independent profit-oriented operators will prefer to provide services mainly in densely populated areas where ambulance travel times are short. Further, private operators will likely prefer not to operate on the market of emergency transport, which requires costly investments in equipment and qualified personnel and will thus engage in a form of "cherry-picking." Finally, because the public ambulance service has a legal obligation to provide service 24 hours a day and throughout an entire territory, any resulting reduction of revenue of the public ambulance service would not be compensated for by a corresponding reduction of its costs. Its costs are largely fixed stand-by costs that do not vary with the amount of services actually provided.

Consequently, a Member State is in principle entitled to reserve both emergency and non-emergency transport to the undertakings that exclusively provide the public ambulance service, unless such service is manifestly unable to satisfy demand (for example, at peak hours).

As for the public authorities responsible for refusing authorization to provide independent ambulance services, the Advocate General concluded that these are not "undertakings" under Article 86(1).

It is settled case law that public bodies offering goods or services may be regarded as undertakings. On the other hand, activities in the exercise of official authority are sheltered from the application of competition rules. An entity acts in the exercise of official authority where the nature and purpose of the activity in question, and the rules to which the entity is subject, are typical of a public authority.

Advocate General Jacobs considered that the grant or refusal of authorization for the provision of ambulance services is clearly an exercise of official authority. Before authorizing it, the authorities examine the safety and efficiency of the operation, the reliability and professional qualifications of the operator and – under the disputed provision – the possible effects of authorization on the public ambulance service. Authorization is thus a typical administrative decision taken in the exercise of discretion usually reserved for public authorities, and is therefore not covered by Article 86(1).

On October 25, the Court of Justice rendered its judgment in the matter.[17] The Court agreed with the Advocate General's holding that medical aid organizations responsible for running public ambulance services are undertakings enjoying special or exclusive rights within the meaning of Article 86 EC. They are entrusted with a task of general economic interest, consisting of an obligation to transport sick or injured persons throughout the territory concerned at uniform rates and on identical conditions as to quality, without regard to individual situations or to the degree of economic profitability of each individual operation.

The Court accepted that the costs of providing the emergency transport service can be offset with revenue from the more profitable service of providing non-emergency transport, but left it to national courts to determine whether the restriction of competition placed on non-emergency patient transport services is necessary to enable medical aid organizations to provide services (in all situations and 24 hours a day) in economically acceptable conditions, and therefore authorized by Article 86(2). The Court added that independent operators should be allowed to operate if medical aid organizations occupying a dominant position are not able to provide transport services in an effective manner.

---

[17] 2001 ECR I-8089.

2.2. ECJ – ORDER

Case C-497/99 Irish Sugar v Commission

On July 10, the Court of Justice rejected Irish Sugar's appeal against a judgment of the Court of First Instance of October 7, 1999, which had upheld the Commission's finding that Irish Sugar, the sole processor of sugar beet and the principal supplier of sugar in Ireland, infringed Article 82 EC by abusing its dominant position on the retail sugar market in Ireland.[18]

Irish Sugar contested, among other things, the finding of the Court of First Instance that it held with SDL, which was 51%-owned by Irish Sugar, a collective dominant position on the retail sugar market between 1985 and February 1990. Although Irish Sugar did not make the day-to-day decisions of SDL, the Court found that the factors connecting the two companies gave them the ability to adopt a common market policy. Those factors included Irish Sugar's representation on the board of SDL, the direct economic ties constituted by SDL's commitment to obtain its supplies exclusively from Irish Sugar, and the latter's financing of all consumer promotions and rebates offered by SDL to its customers. Interestingly, Irish Sugar and SDL operated in vertically related markets.

Irish Sugar argued that, besides the above factors, a finding of collective dominance required that the companies in question also be found to have adopted the same commercial strategy. Irish Sugar added that, by examining whether the companies concerned *had the power* to adopt a common market policy, the Court of First Instance had failed to make the necessary *ex post* assessment, and instead examined the behavior of the companies *ex ante*.

The Court rejected Irish Sugar's claims, and repeated the principle established in *Compagnie Maritime Belge* that collective dominance requires an examination of the economic links or factors giving rise to a connection between the undertakings concerned, and whether such links *enable* the undertakings to act together independently of their competitors, their customers and consumers.

As the Court of Justice stated in *Compagnie Maritime Belge*,[19] while the mere fact that two or more undertakings are linked by an agreement or a concerted practice within the meaning of Article 81(1) does not itself constitute a sufficient basis for a finding of collective dominance, such agreement or concerted practice

---

[18] 2001 ECR I-5333.

[19] Joined Cases C-395/96 P and C-396/96 P 2000 ECR I-1365.

may result in the undertakings concerned being so linked as to their conduct on a particular market that they present themselves as a collective entity *vis-à-vis* their competitors, trading partners and consumers. In any event, the existence of an agreement or other links in law is not indispensable to a finding of a collective dominant position; such a finding may be based on other connecting factors and would depend on an economic assessment, in particular of the structure of the market in question.

2.3. COMMISSION – DECISIONS

Deutsche Post

On March 20, the Commission concluded its antitrust investigation into Deutsche Post (DP) with a decision finding that the German postal operator abused its dominant position by granting fidelity rebates and engaging in predatory pricing.[20] This is the first formal Commission decision in the postal sector under Article 82 EC.

The Commission found DP to be dominant in the German market for mail-order parcels. This market was found to be distinct from the markets for over-the-counter parcels and B-to-B parcels. Between 1990 and 1999, DP had a stable volume-based share of the mail-order parcel market exceeding 85%.

Fidelity rebates. The Commission's investigation revealed that from 1974 through October 2000, DP gave substantial discounts to its large mail-order customers on the condition that the customer send a sizable proportion of its mail-order parcels via DP. According to the Commission, by granting fidelity rebates to its biggest partners, DP deliberately prevented competitors from reaching the "critical mass" (estimated at an annual turnover of 100 million parcels) to enter the German mail-order delivery market successfully.

In light of the fact that fidelity rebates given by an undertaking in a dominant position constitute a serious infringement of Article 82 repeatedly condemned by the Community courts, and given the long duration of the scheme in the case at issue, the Commission imposed a fine of € 24 million for the abuse.

Predatory pricing. The Commission found that DP was "cross-subsidizing" its business parcel services by using revenues from its profitable letter-mail business,

---

[20] OJ 2001 L 125/27.

in which it enjoys a monopoly, to finance a strategy of below-cost selling in business parcel services, which are open to competition.

Cross-subsidization occurs where the earnings from a given service do not suffice to cover the incremental costs of providing that service, and where there is another service whose earnings exceed its stand-alone costs. Those earnings are then used to finance the under-performing service.

The Commission's decision also establishes a test for determining whether cross-subsidies qualify as predatory pricing. Prices charged by a monopoly for its services in a sector open to competition have to cover at least the additional cost incurred in branching out into the competitive sector. According to the Commission, these additional, or "incremental," costs are those incurred in providing a specific parcel service. They do not include common fixed costs.

When calculating the share of the common fixed costs, it must be borne in mind that DP has a "universal service obligation" to maintain a capacity reserve large enough to cover any peak demands for over-the-counter parcel services while meeting statutory quality standards for those services. Even if DP were no longer to offer mail-order parcel services, it would still be obliged to provide catalogues and parcels over the counter within a specified delivery target. This obligation to maintain a reserve capacity is known in economic terms as the "carrier of last resort." By contrast, a private firm, such as UPS (the complainant in this case), may cut back on staff and equipment in proportion to a reduction in volume.

Having analyzed the distribution between common fixed costs and costs that are attributable to a particular service provided by DP, the Commission examined whether the average incremental costs per item for mail-order parcel services were covered by revenues. The investigation revealed that they were not, for a period of five years. This means that every sale by DP in the mail-order parcel services business during that period represented a loss comprising all the capacity maintenance costs and at least part of the additional costs of providing the service.

The Commission decided not to impose a fine for this abuse, since the economic cost concepts used to identify predatory activity were not sufficiently developed at the time the abuse occurred. Furthermore, DP tackled the issue in a satisfactory way by undertaking to create a separate company supplying business parcel services. The system of transparent and market-based pricing between DP and the new entity for products and services they might provide to one another would be a suitable safeguard against the use of revenues from the monopoly market to finance such services.

Note that the decision does not necessarily establish a new rule for predatory pricing. The decision merely clarifies the Commission's position on the costs to be covered by a multi-product monopoly operator that offers an additional line of

Part I: EC Competition Developments

products in markets open to competition. In such cases, it is extremely difficult to allocate the common costs between the monopoly sector and the competitive sector.

Duales System Deutschland AG

On April 20, the Commission decided that Duales System Deutschland AG (DSD) abused its dominant position in the market for organizing the collection and recycling of sales packaging in Germany.[21]

DSD was the only company operating a country-wide system of collecting and recycling packaging waste in Germany; it created the "Green Dot" trademark for use in this system. The German Packaging Ordinance as well as Directive 94/62 on packaging and packaging waste require manufacturers and distributors to take back, free of charge, used sales packaging from consumers at or near the point of sale. Manufacturers and distributors adhering to a comprehensive collection system like the one offered by DSD are exempted from this obligation. Since DSD operates the only comprehensive collection system in Germany, undertakings wishing to be exempted from the collecting obligations under German law must use DSD's services.

The Commission objected to a provision in agreements between DSD and its customers providing that customers have to pay fees corresponding to the volume of packaging bearing the Green Dot trademark, rather than fees corresponding to the volume of packaging for which DSD is actually providing a take-back and recycling service. DSD thus linked the fee payable under the agreements not to the use of the service provided by it, but solely to the use of the Green Dot trademark, whether or not the recycling services of DSD are also being used. The Commission found this to be abusive, since it *de facto* prevented undertakings from using competing systems (what the Commission identified as 'obstructive abuse'). Customers that wanted to use, for some of their sales packaging, services provided by competitors of DSD, would have had to either pay a double fee (to DSD for the trademark and for DSD's competitors for the service) or separate their production and distribution so that some products would bear the Green Dot trademark (and would be collected and recycled by DSD) and others would not (and would be

---

[21] OJ 2002 L 166/1; see also proceedings related to Article 81 EC, OJ 2001 L 319/1 and appeal to CFI, Case T-289/01 *Der Grüne Punkt – Duales System Deutschland v Commission* OJ 2002 C 44/18.

recycled by DSD's competitors). In addition, the Commission considered that DSD imposed unreasonable prices and commercial terms on its customers ('exploitative abuse'). The Commission considered that the conduct of DSD went beyond what is necessary to protect the essential function of its Green Dot trademark.

Following the Commission's decision, DSD may no longer charge a fee for that part of the sales packaging bearing the Green Dot trademark for which it can be shown that the take-back and recovery obligation, as set out in the German packaging ordinance, has been properly fulfilled, either by another party or through a self-management solution. While the Commission stated that it would normally levy a fine on an undertaking that had abused its dominant position in this way, it has not imposed a fine in this case, continuing its practice of not imposing fines against an undertaking that could not easily assess, on the basis of previous decisions of the Commission or the courts, the compatibility of its behavior with competition rules.

DSD appealed the Commission's decision to the Court of First Instance, maintaining that it violates DSD's trademark rights because it effectively compels DSD to allow manufacturers and distributors to use its Green Dot trademark free of charge, even when they rely on the services of DSD's competitors. It thus prevents the trademark from identifying the sales packaging that is eliminated by DSD's system. DSD also argued that its trademark is not indispensable for manufacturers or distributors wishing to adhere to other systems. On November 15, the President of the Court of First Instance rejected DSD's request to suspend execution of the Commission's decision, finding that an injunction was unnecessary to prevent irreparable harm to DSD.[22] While the Court did not need to determine in these interim proceedings whether the Commission was right to conclude that Article 82 was breached, it did make clear that an intellectual property right holder has the power to restrict competition in order to protect the specific subject matter of the right. Therefore, it would have to be examined, according to the Court, whether the royalty regime imposed by the holder of a trademark right may be justified by the need to protect the specific subject matter of that right, *i.e.*, whether the provisions of the agreements concluded by DSD go beyond what is necessary to protect the essential function of the trademark right.

---

[22] Case T-151/01R *Der Grüne Punkt – Duales System Deutschland AG v Commission* OJ 2002 C 68/11.

IMS HEALTH

On July 3, the Commission issued an interim measures decision finding that, by refusing to license its intellectual property to competitors, IMS HEALTH (IMS) abused its dominant position on the market for regional pharmaceutical sales data services in Germany.[23] IMS is a market research company that purchases data that record sales to pharmacies from pharmaceutical wholesalers. IMS then provides this data to pharmaceutical companies, which use it mainly to monitor and assess the performance of their sales representatives.

Regional sales data is provided as a grid superimposed on a country map, grouping communities of doctors, pharmacies and patients. It is developed on the basis of publicly available data, such as postal codes and distribution of physicians and pharmacies. Segmentation allows sales data to be broken down into small, useful geographic areas called "bricks", while at the same time, to protect the privacy of certain data, not identifying sales to individual pharmacies. In Germany, IMS has a copyright on its structure, which contains 1,860 bricks.

The Commission did not contest the validity of IMS's copyright, but found that it is *prima facie* illegal for IMS to refuse to license its copyrighted brick structure to its principal competitors in Germany. The Commission considered that an abuse relating to the exercise of an intellectual property right exists if: (i) the refusal of access to the facility is likely to eliminate all competition in the relevant market; (ii) such refusal is not capable of being objectively justified; and (iii) the facility is indispensable to carry on business because there is no actual or potential substitute in existence for it.

The brick structure is the industry standard, as confirmed by the pharmaceutical companies that assisted in its development. The Commission therefore noted that parties wishing to offer regional sales data services in Germany cannot realistically use an alternative that would not infringe IMS's copyright. The Commission views these as "exceptional circumstances", justifying compulsory licensing in accordance with the principles established by the Court of Justice in *Magill*.[24]

The Commission concluded that IMS's refusal to license could not be objectively justified, and that there was a likelihood of serious and irreparable harm to IMS's competitors and the public interest.

---

[23] OJ 2002 L 59/19; final report of the Hearing Officer OJ 2002 C 53/7.

[24] Joined Cases C-241/91 P and C-242/91 P *Radio Telefis Eireann (RTE) and Independent Televisions Publications (ITP) v Commission* 1995 ECR I-743.

The Commission therefore ordered IMS to license the copyright "without delay" to third parties present on the German market at a mutually-agreed royalty rate (or failing such agreement, at a rate determined by an independent expert) to permit them to supply data services based on IMS's brick structure.

Deutsche Post

On July 25, the Commission condemned Deutsche Post for abusing its dominant position on the German market for the delivery of international mail.[25] The abusive conduct involved interception, surcharge and delay of international mail from the United Kingdom arriving in Germany. Deutsche Post considered any incoming international mail containing a reference to Germany (usually in the form of a German reply address) as having been sent from within Germany, regardless of where the mail was produced or posted. Deutsche Post thus intercepted and refused to deliver the mailings, unless the full German domestic tariff was paid.

The Commission found that Deutsche Post abused its dominant market position by: (i) refusing to supply its delivery service, in that the Post refused to deliver the mailings on terms that would be acceptable to the sender (constructive refusal to supply); (ii) discriminating between international mail which Deutsche Post considered genuine and international mail which it incorrectly considered to be domestic (charging more for the latter, even though the service provided by Deutsche Post in both cases was the same); (iii) charging excessive prices, given that the price charged by Deutsche Post for delivering international mail, which Deutsche Post incorrectly considered domestic, had no reasonable relationship to real costs or to the real value of the service provided; and (iv) limiting markets, given that the interceptions, surcharges and delays limited directly the output on the German market for delivery of international mail. In the long run, dissatisfied customers were discouraged from using postal operators in the United Kingdom for mail addressed to final destinations in Germany.

In reaching its conclusions, the Commission observed that reply addresses cannot always be relied on in order to determine the origin of the mailings. Bulk mailings are often distributed to addressees in a number of countries from one distribution point. Experience shows that, since response rates to commercial mailings are much higher if customers can send their replies to an address in their own country, it is crucial to have a local reply address in each country of

---

[25] OJ 2001 L 331/34; final report of the Hearing Officer OJ 2001 C 358/5.

distribution. If these reply addresses were treated as the real sender's address, and thus intercepted, the development of centralized mailing solutions in the EU could be impeded.

The Commission imposed a fine of only € 1,000 on Deutsche Post because, first, Deutsche Post undertook to stop intercepting, surcharging or delaying international mail of the type in question, even in cases where there might be doubts as to its origins. Second, the behavior of Deutsche Post had been condoned by German courts for a number of years. Third, EC competition rules concerning this type of mail were unclear at the time when the majority of the interceptions took place, and there was no directly applicable EC case law.

La Poste France

On October 23, the Commission found that France had infringed Article 86 EC by failing to monitor properly La Poste's activities in the mail delivery market, in which it enjoys a monopoly, while competing with other undertakings in the mail preparation market.[26] French mail preparation firms provide a variety of services ranging from the production and assembly of large mail distributions to the delivery of pre-sorted mail to La Poste.

Article 86 prohibits national measures relating to public undertakings or undertakings enjoying exclusive rights that would lead them to abuse their dominant position.[27]

Most of the mail that preparation firms handle is ultimately distributed by La Poste, which can define the financial and technical conditions on which competitors may have access to its distribution network. La Poste's monopoly gives rise to a potential conflict of interest, in that it is in a position to discriminate against competitors in the mail preparation market by amending tariffs, defining technical standards in such a way as to eliminate certain mail preparation firms, or applying them differently to different firms.

The Commission found that France insufficiently monitored La Poste's activities, including the contracts it entered into with its commercial partners. French legislation provides for only partial scrutiny of the conditions that La Poste applies to mail preparation firms. The Ministry responsible for monitoring La Poste's

---

[26] OJ 2002 L 61/32; final report of the Hearing Officer OJ 2002 C 55/32.

[27] See Case C-260/89 *ERT* 1991 ECR I-2925.

activities also safeguards the financial interests of the State in La Poste. The Commission considered that this might affect the Ministry's impartiality.

France announced during the proceedings that it intended to create an ombudsman empowered to issue public and reasoned opinions and to intervene in the relations between La Poste and its customers and partners. The Commission considered that this would represent a very significant advance, subject to a number of changes and adjustments to enhance the independence and effectiveness of the monitoring activities.

This decision demonstrates the Commission's ongoing concern that there be adequate and independent regulatory supervision of legal monopolies.

2.4. COMMISSION – GUIDELINES

Draft Guidelines on Market Analysis and the Calculation of Significant Market Power for Electronic Communications Networks and Services

The Commission adopted draft guidelines in advance of the final adoption of a new regulatory regime for electronic communications services.[28] The draft guidelines are based on existing case law and the Commission's own practice in the field of electronic communications markets. The draft guidelines will be discussed with the national regulatory and national competition authorities and with parties concerned. Definitive guidelines will be adopted by the Commission when the Council and the European Parliament formally adopt the framework directive.[29]

On July 12, 2000, the Commission proposed a directive for a new regulatory framework for electronic communications services and networks. Article 13 of the proposed framework directive defines undertakings with "significant market power" based on the concept of "dominant position" of Article 82 EC. Article 14 of the proposed directive also provides that the Commission will adopt guidelines on market definition and the calculation of significant market power to provide guidance to the national regulatory authorities in the application of this new concept.

---

[28] COM 2001/175 March 28, 2001; Commission Press Release IP/01/456 March 28, 2001.

[29] Parliament and Council Directive 2002/21 on a common regulatory framework for electronic communications networks and services was ultimately adopted on February 14, 2002. OJ 2002 L 108/33. However, as of publication, definitive guidelines have not yet been adopted.

Part I: EC Competition Developments

Importance of market shares. The guidelines reaffirm that undertakings with market shares of no more than 25% do not enjoy a dominant position. Dominance concerns normally arise only in the case of undertakings with market shares of over 40%, and extremely large market shares (in excess of 50%) are in themselves, save in exceptional circumstances, evidence of the existence of dominant positions. Nonetheless, the guidelines provide that an undertaking with a large market share may be presumed to have significant market power, that is, to be in a dominant position, only if its market share has remained stable over time. The fact that an undertaking with a significant position on the market is gradually losing market share may indicate that the market is becoming more competitive, but it does not preclude a finding of significant market power. By the same token, fluctuating market shares over time may be indicative of a lack of market power in the relevant market.

The guidelines suggest that in the telecommunications sector, where an operator often has a dominant position on the infrastructure market and a significant presence on the downstream (*i.e.*, services) market, it might be appropriate to find that such operator has significant market power on both markets taken together.

Market entry. A finding of dominance also depends on an assessment of ease of market entry. According to the guidelines, in the telecommunications sector, barriers to entry are often high because of existing legislative and other regulatory requirements which may limit the number of available licences or the provision of certain services. Furthermore, barriers to entry exist where entry into the relevant market requires large investments and the programming of capacities over a long time in order to be profitable.

Collective dominance. The Commission considers that it follows from the recent jurisprudence of the Court of Justice and Court of First Instance in *Compagnie Maritime Belge* and *Gencor*[30] that, although the existence of structural links can be relied upon to support a finding of a collective dominant position, such a finding can also be made in relation to an oligopolistic or highly concentrated market, the structure of which is, by itself, conducive to coordinated effects. In addition, in applying the notion of collective dominance, national authorities may also take into consideration decisions adopted under Regulation 4064/89 in the

---

[30] Joined Cases C-395/96 P and C-396/96 P 2000 ECR I-1365; Case T-102/96 1999 ECR II-0753.

telecommunications sector, in which the Commission has examined whether any of the notified transactions could give rise to a finding of collective or oligopolistic dominance.

Essential facilities. As regards the notion of "essential facilities," the guidelines note that there is for the moment no jurisprudence in relation to the electronic communications sector. In other contexts, this notion is only relevant with regard to the existence of an abuse of a dominant position under Article 82 and has no bearing on the *ex ante* assessment of significant market power within the meaning of the framework directive.

3. MERGERS AND ACQUISITIONS

3.1. NOTICE

Notice on Remedies

On March 2, the Commission published a notice adopted in late 2000 on remedies acceptable under Council Regulation 4064/89 and Commission Regulation 447/98.[31] Remedies (also known as commitments or undertakings) have become an important element of the merger control process, with a significant recent increase in conditional "Phase I" clearances and ever-more complex remedy proposals in "Phase II" proceedings. The notice is intended to provide guidance on the substantive and procedural considerations faced by parties proposing to offer remedies in order to facilitate regulatory clearance under the Merger Control Regulation.

The notice largely codifies 10 years of Commission experience in dealing with remedies under the Merger Control Regulation. The most important innovation in the notice is its recognition of the Commission's recent application of the up-front buyer concept (also known as the "fix-it-first" principle).

Restorative effect on competition. Where the Commission identifies a notified transaction as likely to create or strengthen a dominant position that would significantly impede competition in the common market, the burden rests on the notifying parties to propose remedies that would eliminate such concerns and "restore conditions of effective competition in the common market on a lasting basis."

Preference for divestitures. The notice confirms the Commission's preference for structural remedies, usually involving the divestiture of assets, rather than behavioral commitments that may require ongoing monitoring. Non-structural remedies are not excluded, however, but will be evaluated on a case-by-case basis. The Commission's preference for divestitures is especially marked during the initial

---

[31] OJ 2001 C 68/3.

Phase I investigation, since commitments at this stage will be accepted only if the competition issue is "so straightforward and the remedies so clear-cut" as to exclude clearly serious doubts and thus obviate the need for a second-stage inquiry.

Divestiture. The notice underlines that activities to be divested must consist of "a viable business that, if operated by a suitable purchaser, can compete effectively with the merged entity. Normally a viable business is an existing one that can operate on a stand-alone-basis." Once a divestiture is made a condition of clearance, the notice identifies situations in which the parties may add other assets to the original package to increase its attractiveness to buyers. In some cases, alternative divestiture commitments involving sale of either one or another business, or the removal of structural links between competitors, may be the appropriate remedy.

Non-structural remedies. As discussed, the Commission's preference is for structural remedies. The notice does, however, contain a non-exhaustive list of other types of remedies that may be appropriate where the divestiture of a business is impossible or disproportionate. In this regard, the notice identifies termination of exclusive agreements and licensing arrangements to provide access to infrastructure or key technology as possible remedies. Remedy packages combining divestiture and various other types of remedies may in certain circumstances be necessary to prevent market foreclosure (*e.g.*, in the media and telecoms sectors).

Cases where remedies are difficult or impossible. Where no suitable remedies can be found, or where proposed remedies are so extensive and complex that their restorative effect on competition cannot be determined with sufficient certainty, the transaction will be prohibited.

Submission of remedies in Phases I and II. The notice emphasizes the importance of the statutory deadlines for negotiating remedies. The deadline for submission of remedies in Phase I is three weeks after receipt of the notification. Where parties submit commitments together, the Commission's deadline for issuing a Phase I clearance (or launching a second-stage inquiry) is extended from one month to six weeks. The deadline for submission of remedies in a four-month Phase II inquiry is the end of the third month following the initiation of Phase II. An extension to the Phase II deadline is possible only in "exceptional circumstances and where … there is sufficient time to make a proper assessment of the proposal and to allow adequate consultation with Member States and third parties."

Implementation of remedies. The notice contains guidance on the implementation of divestment commitments. The matters covered include a description of: (i) essential features of the commitments (*i.e.*, precise and exhaustive definition of the relevant business, completion in a fixed time period, purchaser to be an independent existing or potential competitor whose acquisition raises no new competition issues); (ii) interim preservation of the business by appointment of a "hold separate trustee"; (iii) implementation through a divestiture trustee; (iv) approval of the trustee and the trustee mandate; and (v) approval of the purchaser and the purchase agreement. Many of these principles apply equally to other types of remedies.

Up-front buyer principle. The notice provides that, "where the viability of the divestiture package depends ... to a large extent on the identity of the purchaser," the parties may be required to commit not to close the notified transaction before reaching a binding agreement to sell the business to a purchaser approved by the Commission. This principle, which has become a common feature of U.S. merger proceedings, was first invoked by the Commission only recently in a situation where it was uncertain whether a suitable purchaser could be found capable of competing effectively with the merging parties.[32] The notice anticipates that, in future, the Commission may require that a binding sale agreement be concluded with an approved purchaser prior to closing where there is uncertainty whether a suitable buyer exists.

As a practical matter, application of this "fix-it-first" principle may significantly delay the timetable for closing a notified transaction. It may take time for merging parties to negotiate a sale agreement with an approved buyer and, perhaps more significantly, application of the principle could be expected to increase the leverage of third parties, usually competitors, who may succeed in delaying the closing of a transaction by raising doubts as to the suitability of a given buyer.

Given the increasing number of EU merger cases subject to conditional clearance, the guidance provided by the notice is welcome. In particular, the notice provides a useful summary of the principles and procedures applied by the Commission to various merger control scenarios where remedies are considered necessary. It will be interesting to observe whether the most significant change contained in the notice – the up-front buyer principle – will be applied only exceptionally (as the notice seems to suggest) or, following U.S. practice, will develop into a more common feature of EU merger control.

---

[32] Case COMP/M.2060 *Bosch/Rexroth* December 13, 2000.

3.2. PROHIBITION DECISIONS

Metsä Tissue/SCA Mölnlycke

On January 31, the Commission blocked the takeover of Finnish tissue paper manufacturer Metsä Tissue by its Swedish competitor SCA Mölnlycke.[33] This is the 14th prohibition decision since 1990, out of a total of over 1,500 notifications.

The Commission investigated the markets for hygienic tissue products in certain Scandinavian countries. The investigation showed that the proposed transaction would lead to the creation or strengthening of single dominant market positions in 21 tissue paper markets in Sweden, Norway and Denmark, and to the creation of duopolistic dominant positions in two tissue product markets in Finland between the merged entity and the U.S. company Fort James.

The Commission followed the approach taken in *Kimberly Clark/Scott*[34] with respect to the product market definition, dividing products into categories according to single end-use products.[35] Each category was then further subdivided according to distribution channels, such as products supplied to retailers (consumer products) and "away-from-home" products supplied to corporate customers, such as hotels, schools and hospitals. The Commission further concluded that, in the field of consumer products, branded products and private labels constitute separate product markets. Both parties own strong brands in the respective end-product categories.

The decision underlines the importance the Commission attributes to effects of relative price changes in defining the product market. This was crucial when the Commission assessed whether competition (i) between private labels and brands on the downstream level, or (ii) between tissue end-use products and end-use products made of other fibers, could result in a broader product market definition.

The Commission noted that competition of private labels with branded products on the downstream level for consumer products was insufficient to include

---

[33] OJ 2002 L 57/1. The proposed merger was part of an extensive exchange of assets between Metsä-Serla and Svenska Cellulosa AB, the parent company of SCA. Two other deals, the acquisitions of Metsä Corrugated by SCA and Modo Paper by Metsä-Serla, were cleared by the Commission with conditions on August 25, 2000, and August 4, 2000, respectively.

[34] OJ 1996 L 183/1.

[35] Including products such as toilet paper, kitchen towels, handkerchiefs and napkins.

Part I: EC Competition Developments

both in one single product market. The Commission concluded that the test of whether consumers would switch to other products in case of a price increase of 5-10% (the so-called SSNIPP test, which is usually applied to define the relevant product market) did not work with respect to the downstream level, as a price increase at the supplier level would not necessarily result in a price increase at the downstream level for consumer products. The Commission found that retailers appeared willing to reduce their margins instead of passing on price increases.

The Commission also noted that end-use products made of tissue and other fibers, *e.g.*, textile wipes, competed primarily on quality or hygiene and not price. The Commission therefore concluded that, according to the SSNIPP test, these products do not fall within the same product market.

Furthermore, the Commission confirmed its approach in *Kimberly Clark/Scott* by rejecting a Europe-wide market definition. The Commission considered the relevant geographic market as national in Sweden, Denmark, Norway and Finland. One element limiting the geographic market was transport costs, since tissue products, which are relatively bulky, can be economically transported over distances of only approximately 800-1,000 kilometers.

In addition, the Commission based part of its geographic market definition, namely the question of homogenous conditions of competition, on the merged entity's prospective geographic scope. The Commission argued that the market in question did not comprise a larger territory (such as the entire Nordic region) because the merged entity would have been in the position to price discriminate among its customers in different Member States.

The Commission set out two general conditions under which price discrimination is likely: (i) it must be possible to identify clearly the area to which an individual customer belongs at the moment of selling it the relevant products; and (ii) trade among customers or arbitrage by third parties should not be feasible. The Commission noted that arbitrage is particularly difficult in cases where the product is sold on a delivered basis and the transportation costs amount to a significant percentage of the final costs.

The Commission's investigation showed that the combined parties' market shares were very high (up to 90% in some of the markets concerned). The Commission concluded that Nordic supermarkets' countervailing buyer power would be insufficient to restrain the merged company's market power, since switching to competitors did not constitute a realistic threat given the insufficient capacity of the parties' competitors to satisfy customers' needs. Moreover, the Commission found high barriers to entry due to high investment costs in terms of building capacity and introducing a new brand.

The parties re-submitted undertakings in second phase that they had already offered unsuccessfully in first phase, including the divestiture of certain assets. The Commission rejected these, arguing that they did not address any of the competition issues identified for consumer and "away-from-home" tissue products in Finland, or for private-label consumer tissue products in Denmark. Furthermore, the Commission considered that the proposed divestment package contained insufficient capacity in a number of product markets for the buyer of that capacity to compete effectively with the merged entity, and to effectively restrain SCA's market power.

General Electric/Honeywell

On July 3, the Commission adopted its 15th prohibition decision under the Merger Regulation when it blocked the proposed acquisition by General Electric Company (GE) of Honeywell International Inc.[36]

The proposed transaction would have combined GE's strong position in the market for aircraft engines with Honeywell's similarly strong position in avionics and non-avionics (such as weather turbulence detection products, collision avoidance and flight management systems, and so-called "black boxes"). This combination would have been further strengthened by GE's leasing and financial arms, GE Capital and GE Capital Aviation Services (GECAS). GECAS is, according to the Commission, the largest purchaser of aircraft, ahead of any airline.

The proposed transaction required authorization from both the U.S. and European antitrust authorities. After carrying out a five-month investigation, the U.S. Department of Justice (DOJ) was concerned that the proposed merger would likely have resulted in higher prices, lower quality and reduced innovation for the U.S. military and a range of commercial business aircraft users. To resolve its antitrust concerns, the DOJ required the parties to divest Honeywell's helicopter engine business and to authorize a third party to provide maintenance, repair and overhaul services for certain models of Honeywell's aircraft engines and auxiliary power units that produce onboard electricity. On May 2, the DOJ announced that it had reached an agreement in principle with GE and Honeywell resolving its concerns.[37]

GE and Honeywell notified the proposed merger to the Commission on February 5. In its first phase investigation, the Commission identified possible horizon-

---

[36] Commission Press Release IP/01/939 July 3, 2001.

[37] Department of Justice Press Release May 2, 2001.

tal overlaps in the market for large regional jet engines. The Commission was also concerned with the merged entity's ability to bundle its products and use combined product offerings to extend existing dominant positions to other markets. Other concerns about the proposed merger involved anti-competitive effects resulting from vertical foreclosure of competing engine, avionics and non-avionics suppliers. Accordingly, the Commission opened a full investigation of the proposed merger on March 1.[38]

On June 14, the deadline for proposing remedial relief, the merging parties submitted proposing divestitures worth $2.2 billion to gain regulatory approval. The Commission also asked for a commitment to modify the commercial behavior of GECAS.[39] According to the Commission, GECAS has conditioned the purchase or financing of aircraft on equipping the aircraft with GE engines. The Commission was concerned that this commercial behavior, if extended to Honeywell products, could create or strengthen dominant positions for these products.

On June 29, Honeywell's CEO, Michael R. Bonsignore, requested GE in a public letter to revise the undertakings submitted on June 14. In particular, he requested that a commitment be submitted under which 19.9% of GECAS's common equity would be privately placed on terms satisfying the governance concerns described by the Commission. This proposal was in response to a June 28 statement by Commissioner Monti that a divestiture of 19.9% of GECAS, combined with the divestitures proposed on June 14, would be sufficient to satisfy the Commission's concerns (and that, in fact, smaller divestitures could have been sufficient). As compensation for the partial spin-off of GECAS, Honeywell offered to reduce the exchange ratio provided for in the merger agreement from 1.055 GE shares for every Honeywell share to 1.01 GE shares. On the same day, GE's CEO, John F. Welch, Jr., rejected Honeywell's offer.

On July 3, the Commission prohibited the proposed merger. The Commission explained that the proposed merger would have severely reduced competition in the aerospace industry and resulted ultimately in higher prices for customers, particularly airlines. The Commission held that it would have created dominant positions in the markets for the supply of avionics, non-avionics and corporate jet engines, and strengthened GE's existing dominant positions in jet engines for large commercial and regional jets. Dominance would have resulted from horizontal overlaps in the market for large regional aircraft engines, the extension of GE's

---

[38] Commission Press Release IP/01/298 March 1, 2001.

[39] Commission Press Release IP/01/842 June 14, 2001.

financial power and vertical integration with Honeywell's products, and the combination of GE's and Honeywell's respective complementary products. The Commission found that such integration would have enabled the merged entity to leverage the respective market power of one party into the products of the other party, thereby foreclosing competitors, eliminating competition and ultimately adversely affecting product quality, services and consumer prices. At a press conference on July 3, Commissioner Monti stated that the role of bundling theories was "fairly limited in the competition assessment of the case" and that "vertical concerns [were among] the key concerns." Furthermore, he clarified that discussions with the parties on remedies confirmed that GECAS would have played a crucial role in the merged entity and that GE was not able to sufficiently modify GECAS's buying policies.

With regard to cooperation with the U.S. antitrust authorities, the Commissioner stressed that both the Commission and the DOJ had been working closely together but that each authority had to perform its assessment independently. He stated that such independent assessment might lead to different interpretations of facts and different forecasts of the anti-competitive effects of a proposed transaction. Notwithstanding the different views of each authority on the proposed merger, the Commissioner once again stated his commitment and determination to strengthen bilateral cooperation in the future and to try to reduce further the risk of dissenting opinions in the antitrust assessment of merger cases.

Schneider Electric/Legrand

On October 10, the Commission prohibited Schneider's acquisition of Legrand due to significant overlaps, particularly in France, in their activities in the electrical equipment sector, which would have resulted in combined market shares ranging between 40% and 90%.[40]

On the last day for submission of commitments, Schneider submitted undertakings, which the Commission found to be inadequate. Schneider then submitted another set of "last-minute" undertakings. The Commission noted that it can only accept such late commitments if it is immediately satisfied, without any doubt, that they would restore the conditions of competition. This was not the case here.

The Commission's prohibition placed Schneider in an unusually difficult position, because it had launched a public exchange offer, closed during the

---

[40] Commission Press Release IP/01/1393 October 10, 2001.

Part I: EC Competition Developments

Commission's second phase investigation, resulting in Schneider's holding around 98% of Legrand's shares at the time of the prohibition decision. Under French law, a public offer cannot be made conditional upon regulatory, including antitrust, approval. Art. 7(3) of the Merger Regulation allows, by way of exception, the launch of public takeover or exchange bids prior to a Commission decision, provided that the voting rights attached to the shares are not exercised before the final Commission decision.

On January 30, 2002, the Commission ordered Schneider under Art. 8(4) of the Merger Regulation to separate from Legrand.[41] To ensure Schneider's incentive to compete actively with Legrand and to restore effective competition, the Commission prohibited Schneider from retaining a participation exceeding 5% in Legrand, and mandated that Legrand remain intact. The Commission allowed the parties to decide how to separate Schneider and Legrand. Schneider could, for instance, sell its stake to a third party or refloat its Legrand shares on the stock market. Under the first option, the Commission would need to approve the buyer, examining its viability and independence. The deadline given for the separation remains confidential.

Tetra Pak/Sidel

On October 30, the Commission prohibited Tetra Pak's acquisition of Sidel.[42] Tetra Pak is active in carton packaging. Sidel is the leading manufacturer of polyethylene terephthalate (PET) packaging equipment, in particular stretch blow-moulding machines (SBMs).

The Commission found that the combination of the dominant company in carton packaging, which has a market share exceeding 80%, with the leading company in PET packaging equipment would result in (i) the creation of a dominant position in the EEA market for PET packaging equipment, in particular SBMs used for "sensitive products" (those sensitive to light or oxygen, *e.g.*, liquid dairy products, fruit juices, iced tea and coffee drinks), and (ii) the strengthening of Tetra Pak's dominant position in the EEA market for aseptic carton packaging equipment and aseptic cartons.

The Commission found that there are four major packaging materials used for liquid food packaging: cartons, plastic (including PET and high-density poly-

---

[41] Commission Press Release IP/02/173 January 30, 2002.
[42] Commission Press Release IP/01/1516 October 30, 2001.

ethylene (HDPE)), cans and glass. While acknowledging that carton and PET packaging equipment currently belong to distinct product markets, the Commission nevertheless considered them to be closely-related markets belonging to the same industrial sector, namely liquid food packaging. It further considered PET and cartons to be substitutes, usable for common product segments. The Commission also found that PET use for sensitive products will significantly grow in the coming years.

The Commission concluded that the merger would provide the new entity with the ability and incentive to leverage its dominant position in cartons to gain a dominant position in PET packaging equipment. The Commission envisaged possible leveraging in two ways: (i) customers needing both carton and PET equipment could be forced or encouraged to obtain both sorts of equipment from a single supplier, or (ii) the new entity could pressure customers or provide incentives (predatory pricing or loyalty rebates) for them to buy Sidel SBMs. Even if such leverage could be applied only in a minor sector, that of sensitive product PET packaging equipment, the Commission pointed out that this would likely have the effect of barring competitors from the entire sensitive product packaging sector, since they would have no incentive to invest in the complex technology required. In addition, only the PET segment is expected to grow in the future, making it a key market sector.

The Commission also found that competitors in the closely-related carton and PET packaging equipment markets exercise significant competitive pressure on each other. In particular, it noted that PET packaging exerted a competitive constraint on Tetra Pak's carton packaging business, because customers would likely switch to PET packaging following a 20% increase in the price of carton packaging. The disappearance of this competitive constraint would result in a strengthening of Tetra Pak's dominant position in carton packaging.

The Commission's decision of October 17 in *CVC/Lenzing* prohibiting a proposed concentration in the fiber manufacturing sector provides an interesting comparison.[43] In that case, the Commission found that a third-party fiber would not exert an effective competitive constraint on the dominant fiber, even though consumers would likely switch from the dominant fiber to the competing fiber following a 20% increase in the price of the dominant fiber. Thus, it appears that the prospect of customer switching after a 20% price increase is a significant enough constraint that the Commission will not permit its elimination in the context of a

---

[43] Commission Press Release IP/01/1436 October 17, 2001.

concentration, yet not so significant that parties may invoke it as evidence of sufficient competitive constraint on a planned concentration.

3.3. SECOND-PHASE DECISIONS WITH UNDERTAKINGS

EDF/EnBW

On February 7, the Commission authorized the acquisition of joint control of German electricity company Energie Baden-Württemberg AG (EnBW) by Electricité de France (EDF) and Zweckverband Oberschwäbische Elektrizitätswerke, an association of nine southwest German districts.[44]

EDF is a wholly state-owned French company active in all fields of electricity generation, supply and transmission in France. EDF also has shareholdings in electricity companies in many European countries. EnBW is a vertically integrated electricity utility active in all fields of electricity supply and transmission primarily in southwest Germany.

The Commission defined the relevant market as the market for electricity supply to eligible (*i.e.*, large) customers in France.[45] The Commission noted that the relevant market definition was connected to the status of liberalization of the electricity sector in France, as currently only large customers are free to choose their electricity suppliers. In addition, supplies from outside the French territory are low due to technical reasons, as electricity must be imported via inter-connectors with limited capacity.

The investigation showed that, prior to the notified transaction, EDF already enjoyed a dominant position on this market, with a market share of approximately 90%, with only three other electricity producers active in France.[46]

The Commission considered that the initially notified operation would strengthen EDF's dominant position on this market because it would result in: (i) the elimination of EnBW as the strategically best-placed potential competitor on the French market; (ii) an increase of EDF's retaliation potential in Germany; (iii) an increase

---

[44] OJ 2002 L 59/1.

[45] Eligible customers in France are industrial clients that consume more than 16 gigawatt-hours/year (GWh/year).

[46] These are CNR, Société Nationale d'Electricité Thermique (SNET) and Harpen AG, part of the German RWE group. They only have a small share of electricity generation and supply their production mainly to EDF.

of EDF's current foothold in Switzerland through EnBW's controlling shareholding in the major Swiss electricity producer WATT, and the elimination of WATT as a potential competitor on the French market; and (iv) the strengthening of EDF's outstanding position as a pan-European electricity supplier.

The Commission's reasoning in points (ii) and (iv) merits particular attention. The Commission argued that, post-merger, EDF would be capable of using its presence in Germany to deter actual competitors, such as RWE, E.ON and HEW, from aggressively competing for the supply of eligible customers in France. Without having an equivalent presence in France, these companies would be discouraged from aggressively challenging EDF's position there. The Commission based this argument on competitors' statements.

With regard to strengthening EDF's outstanding position as a pan-European supplier, the Commission's investigation showed that demand for pan-European services is likely to increase. As a result of various acquisitions during the last few years, EDF is active in a number of Member States,[47] whereas it is not possible for foreign companies to acquire interests in French electricity generators and/or suppliers. The merger would enable EDF to extend its local presence into Germany and would put it in a unique position to offer Europe-wide services to industrial and commercial customers.

In order to alleviate the Commission's concerns, EDF offered to make electricity generation capacity located in France available to competitors, 5,000 MW in the form of virtual power plants and 1,000 MW in the form of back-to-back agreements to existing co-generation power purchase agreements. This will amount to approximately 30% of the current electricity supplied to eligible customers in France. Competitors will have access to this capacity via auctions conducted by EDF under the supervision of a trustee. This undertaking is envisaged as lasting for five years (with the possibility of extension), to allow the development of alternative supply sources in France.

EDF also undertook to renounce exercising its voting rights in one of the other French electricity generators (CNR) and to withdraw its representative from the CNR board of directors. Finally, the parties committed to divest EnBW's shareholding in Swiss electricity company WATT.

The decision highlights the Commission's intention to use merger proceedings as a tool to liberalize previously state-owned sectors, such as electricity, gas, telecommunications and postal services, a process that has been delayed by the lack of implementation of relevant legislation by the Member States.

---

[47] Including Austria, Italy, Sweden and the United Kingdom.

ADtranz/Bombardier

On April 3, the Commission cleared the takeover of DaimlerChrysler's railway division ADtranz by Canadian Bombardier, subject to conditions.[48] ADtranz is active in the manufacture of rolling stock and signaling equipment. Bombardier is active in the aircraft, rail transportation equipment and recreational product industries.

The transaction creates the world's largest integrated producer of railway equipment, ahead of Alstom and Siemens, the other two main players in the rail equipment industry both in Europe and worldwide. The Commission's investigation focused on the markets for regional trains and trams/light rail vehicles in Germany, in which the Commission found that Bombardier and ADtranz together accounted for more than half of each market during the period 1995-1999. Despite the increasing number of EU-wide tenders, the Commission found that national technical regulations meant that these markets were still national.

Regarding horizontal overlaps, the Commission acknowledged the principle that market shares alone are of limited significance in bidding markets, because they reflect only the activities of the winning bidders and do not show how many credible competitors actually participated as bidders.

The Commission expressed concerns regarding three independent component suppliers in Germany, since Bombardier would become vertically integrated through the transaction. Of these three suppliers, two companies supply electrical propulsion systems for trams and regional trains (Kiepe and Elin) and a third company manufactures mechanical parts for regional trains (Stadler).

To alleviate the vertical foreclosure concerns, the parties offered commitments designed to reduce and shift market share from the merged entity, to support the development of Stadler into a competitive manufacturer and supplier of regional trains and trams/light rail vehicles, and to strengthen the independent propulsion system suppliers' market position, ensuring their viability (and availability for strategic relationships with third-party competitors) after the merger.

With respect to the market for regional trains, the parties offered Stadler an exclusive license in Europe for one of ADtranz's regional trains. Stadler will also obtain full control over the manufacture and marketing of an articulated regional

---

[48] OJ 2002 L 69/50. ADtranz was created in 1995 through the pooling of the rail business activities of ABB and Daimler-Benz (now called DaimlerChrysler), which acquired sole control in 1999.

train developed by Stadler but initially built and marketed in Germany by ADtranz. Interestingly, the Commission treated these commitments as equivalent to a divestiture of ADtranz's product portfolio in regional trains currently sold in Germany.

In addition, Bombardier will terminate a joint venture between Stadler and ADtranz by selling ADtranz's stake to Stadler. For a transitional period, the parties also committed to guarantee capacity for Stadler's German production facility and to supply it with certain components. Bombardier also undertook to divest its minority stake in propulsion supplier Elin and to cooperate continuously with Elin with regard to electrical propulsion for a certain regional train.

With respect to the market for trams/light rail vehicles in Germany, the parties offered an exclusive Europe-wide license of ADtranz's *Variotram* to Stadler. Bombardier also undertook to use Kiepe's traction equipment exclusively for the worldwide sale of a certain tram type for some years, and for the EU-wide sale of tram trains of another type, and to guarantee Kiepe a certain turnover. Bombardier also undertook to cooperate continuously with Elin with regard to electrical propulsion for a particular tram type.

The Commission noted that any further concentration in this sector is likely to require very close scrutiny by the competent competition authorities.

Hidroelectrica del Cantabrico/Villar Mir/EnBW

On September 26, the Commission authorized Villar Mir's and EnBW's acquisition of joint control over Hidroelectrica del Cantabrico, Spain's fourth largest electricity company. EnBW is itself jointly controlled by Electricité de France (EDF) and the German Oberschwäbische Elektrizitätswerke Zweckverband.[49]

The Commission's investigation focused on the national Spanish wholesale market for electricity, and the Commission's concerns related to the strengthening of a dominant position collectively held by Iberdrola and Endesa, the two leading players in this market. The Merger Regulation generally allows the prohibition of a transaction if a third party gains or strengthens a dominant position as a result of a notified transaction. Interestingly, the Commission applied this concept in this case to a collective position held by third parties.

---

49 Commission Press Release IP/01/1320 September 26, 2001. For the Commission's decision approving acquisition of joint control over EnBW by EDF of February 7, 2001, see p. 36.

The Commission found that scarce commercial capacity on the French-Spanish interconnector created a barrier to electricity imports into Spain. The Commission thus argued that, having gained a foothold in Spain and access to Hidrocantabrico's significant generation capacity, EDF would likely resist any increase in the commercial capacity of the interconnector across the Pyrenees. The Commission argued that Iberdrola's and Endesa's collective dominant position would thus have been reinforced in the long term.

To alleviate these concerns, EDF and the operator of the French electricity grid, RTE (a division of EDF), undertook to increase the commercial capacity on the interconnector in question (up to about 4000 MW).

Hutchinson/RMPM/ECT

On November 29, the Commission authorized Hutchinson Netherlands BV's and Rotterdam Municipal Port Management's (RMPM) acquisition of the Rotterdam container terminal operator Europe Combined Terminals BV (ECT) after the parties offered commitments resulting in the creation of independent competition in the Port of Rotterdam.[50] The Commission's second-phase investigation confirmed that the transaction, as originally notified by the parties, would have resulted in the creation of a dominant position in the market for the provision of stevedoring services in respect of the Northern European transshipment market.

The transaction was notified to the Commission in November 1999 as a cooperation agreement under which the parties would jointly acquire all of the shares in ECT. In their notification, which was submitted after the acquisition was completed, the parties applied for an exemption under Article 81. In the course of its investigation, the Commission concluded that the parties should have notified the concentration under the Merger Regulation. It issued a statement of objections in October 2000 laying the grounds for possible fines for an infringement of EC competition rules, in particular for failure to notify and for implementing the acquisition prior to obtaining the Commission's authorization.[51] As a result, the parties decided to notify the transaction under the Merger Regulation in January 2001, while maintaining their view that the operation does not qualify as concentration.[52]

---

[50] Commission Press Release IP/01/1697 November 29, 2001.

[51] Commission Press Release IP/00/1199 October 26, 2000.

[52] Commission Press Release IP/01/295 March 1, 2001.

In its final decision, the Commission did not fine the parties for their failure to notify and implement prior to obtaining proper authorization.[53] In this connection, the Commission stressed that the parties did not attempt to conceal the transaction and that they had been cooperative throughout the Commission's investigation. In reaching its decision, the Commission also took into account the complicated factual and legal analysis required to determine the transaction's proper characterization as concentration under the Merger Regulation.

3.4. SECOND-PHASE DECISIONS WITHOUT UNDERTAKINGS

MAN/Auwärter

On June 20, the Commission authorized the acquisition of Gottlob Auwärter GmbH (Auwärter) by the MAN group; both are German undertakings.[54] Auwärter is active in the production and sale of buses and coaches under the Neoplan brand, and MAN manufactures and markets buses and trucks.

In line with its 1993 *Mercedes/Kässbohrer* decision concerning the bus sector, the Commission defined the relevant markets narrowly, distinguishing between the city-bus market, the market for inter-city buses, and the market for touring coaches. Though it indicated in *Mercedes/Kässbohrer* that the Community procurement rules would lead these markets to evolve into Europe-wide markets, it still defined the current relevant geographic market as national.

The Commission's investigation focused primarily on the city-bus market in Germany. The Commission found that the two main players were MAN and the DaimlerChrysler group through its EvoBus group. EvoBus was the market leader, while Auwärter was a relatively small competitor. The merger would reduce the number of main players from three to two, and MAN/Auwärter and EvoBus would each supply just under half of that market. The Commission's main concern related to possible tacit coordination between MAN/Auwärter and EvoBus and a resulting situation of collective dominance.

However, further investigation showed that a duopoly between MAN and EvoBus in the city-bus market in Germany would not be stable, since only a third of all city buses would be subject to the potential tacit collusion. In addition, the parameters

---

[53] Commission Press Release IP/01/940 July 3, 2001.

[54] OJ 2002 L 116/35.

Part I: EC Competition Developments

of the market were found to exclude mutual control of each other's competitive behavior.

In addition, despite the symmetric market shares of MAN/Auwärter and EvoBus, the Commission concluded that they lacked the structural similarity necessary for a stable duopoly. The Commission based this conclusion primarily on the fact that EvoBus manufactures almost four times as many buses as MAN/Auwärter (and eight times as many buses and trucks, if the DaimlerChrysler group is considered). EvoBus and MAN/Auwärter thus show different cost structures and economies of scale in the city-bus market, where common components (used both for buses and trucks) represent approximately 20% to 30% of the value of an average city bus. This is consistent with the Commission's *Nestlé/Perrier* decision,[55] in which significant cost differences were seen as likely to hinder the implementation of tacit parallel behavior.

Although leading suppliers of a market with symmetric market shares are often expected to have common cost structures, leading to a higher likelihood of collusion and a finding of collective dominance, this decision provides an interesting counterexample.

BASF/Eurodiol/Pantochim

On July 11, the Commission relied on the "failing firm" doctrine to authorize BASF's acquisition of Eurodiol and Pantochim.[56]

Under the failing firm doctrine, which has its origins in U.S. antitrust law, a merger is not likely to create or enhance market power or facilitate its exercise if the target (i) could not meet its financial obligations in the near future, (ii) could not reorganize successfully under the applicable bankruptcy legislation, (iii) would exit the relevant market, absent the merger, and (iv) has made unsuccessful good faith efforts to elicit reasonable alternative offers to acquire its assets that would keep both its tangible and intangible assets in the relevant market and pose a less severe danger to competition than the proposed merger currently being considered.[57]

---

[55] OJ 1992 L 356/1.

[56] Commission Press Release IP/01/984 July 11, 2001.

[57] See § 5.1 of the U.S. Horizontal Merger Guidelines.

In *Kali und Salz*[58] and subsequent cases,[59] the Commission indicated that the failing firm doctrine could be relevant under EC law only if, in addition to the above conditions, the acquiror could show that, absent the acquisition, it would in any event have taken over the target's entire market share.

Referring to the Court of First Instance's judgment in *Kali und Salz* that "[a] merger can be regarded as a rescue merger if the competitive structure resulting from the concentration would deteriorate in similar fashion even if the concentration did not proceed," the Commission recognized in this case that the failing firm doctrine could also be relevant if the exit of the failing firm's assets would likely lead to a greater deterioration of market conditions than following the merger. In allowing the merger, the Commission stressed the exceptional circumstances of this case.

The Commission noted that it applied the failing firm doctrine as articulated in the U.S. Horizontal Merger guidelines, apparently setting aside the additional condition described above by attributing it to the fact that *Kali und Salz* concerned a duopoly, the acquiror and the failing target, and that this condition was therefore "the most obvious method to prove that the concept of 'rescue merger' could be applied to that case."

UPM-Kymmene/Norske Skog/Haindl

On November 21, the Commission authorized UPM-Kymmene's acquisition of Haindl and its simultaneous resale of two of Haindl's six paper mills to Norske Skog.[60]

UPM-Kymmene is the world's largest producer of magazine paper. Norske Skog is the second-largest producer of newsprint in the world. Haindl produces newsprint and magazine paper.

Concerning the EEA newsprint market, the Commission found that UPM-Kymmene/Haindl and the other two major suppliers, Stora Enso and Holmen, would control more than two-thirds of all sales, post-transaction, and examined whether

---

[58] Joined Cases C-68/94 and C-30/95 *France and Société commerciale des potasses et de l'azote (SCPA) and Entreprise Minière et Chimique (EMC) v Commission* 1998 ECR I-1375.

[59] Case IV/M.0890 *Blokker/Toys 'R' Us* OJ 1998 L 316/1; and Case IV/M.0774 *Saint-Gobain/Wacker-Chemie/NOM* OJ 1997 L 247/1.

[60] Commission Press Release IP/01/1629 November 21, 2001.

Part I: EC Competition Developments

the transaction would result in tacit coordination between them, leading to collective dominance. Similarly, in the EEA market for wood-containing magazine paper, the three leading suppliers would control more than two-thirds of all sales, post-transaction.

The Commission examined in particular whether the leading companies would collude tacitly to limit investment in new capacity, and/or to restrict production levels through temporary shut-downs of paper machines to achieve price increases. The Commission's investigation showed, however, that the structure of the newsprint and wood-containing magazine paper markets would not be conducive to such behavior. The markets are characterized by limited stability of market shares, lack of transparency regarding investment in capacity expansion projects and lack of symmetry in cost structures.

Moreover, the Commission found that tacit coordination between the leading suppliers would be difficult to sustain. With respect to the newsprint market, the Commission took into account that Norske Skog has aggressively expanded in the recent past, and another of the three leading suppliers actually consists of two independent companies that are linked through production joint ventures and a common sales organization, but act independently with respect to capacity.

Finally, the Commission pointed out that any attempted price increase by the leading suppliers could be easily undermined by the smaller companies active in both markets, in particular at times when demand for paper is low.

3.5. FIRST-PHASE DECISIONS WITH UNDERTAKINGS

United Airlines/US Air

On January 12, the Commission approved the acquisition of U.S. Airway Group Inc. by UAL Corp., the main operating subsidiary of which is United Airlines Inc.

The Commission concentrated its investigation on the transatlantic flights between the U.S. and Europe operated by the two American companies, in particular on four routes (Frankfurt–Philadelphia, Frankfurt–Charlotte, Frankfurt–Pittsburgh and Munich–Philadelphia).

In line with its *KLM/Alitalia* decision, the Commission defined the relevant market as scheduled flights segmented by routes, *i.e.*, by point-of-origin/point-of-destination city pairs. Each market comprises (i) non-stop flights between the two airports concerned, (ii) non-stop flights between airports whose local service area significantly overlaps with the service area of the airports concerned, and (iii) indirect flights between the airports concerned to the extent that these flights are substitutable for the non-stop flights.

The Commission rejected UAL's submission that the market definition should take into account the impact of the developing network competition with respect to transatlantic flights. The Commission acknowledged that the evolution of carriers on both sides of the Atlantic serving multiple destinations from their respective hubs or gateways, codeshare relationships and alliances affect the supply side of the market. However, the Commission pointed out that, from the demand side, individual city-pairs are not substitutable, and that from the supply side, airlines are not able to start services between all transatlantic city pairs without incurring significant additional costs and risks.

The Commission also specified which indirect flights are included in the above market definition: so-called "competitive indirect flights" are flights which (i) are marketed as connecting flights on the city pair concerned (and thus appear on the computerized reservation system used by travel agents), and (ii) cause only a limited extension of the trip duration. The Commission appears to have accepted third-party input that only flights with a comparable in-flight duration and a connection of no longer than 150 minutes qualify.

Interestingly, the Commission left open whether there is a market for time-sensitive passengers. However, its investigation showed that the distinction between time-sensitive and non-time-sensitive passengers with respect to transatlantic routes is becoming increasingly blurred, as time-sensitive business passengers increasingly buy economy-class tickets and choices of airlines for business passengers tend to be based on corporate discounts instead of travel time.

The Commission concluded that the transaction would substantially reduce the competition previously existing between U.S. Air and Lufthansa on the four routes listed above, because United is a member of the Star Alliance, which in Europe includes, among others, Lufthansa and SAS. In addition, United collaborates with Lufthansa through a transatlantic cooperation agreement. In particular, the Commission found that, on the Frankfurt–Philadelphia route, the operation would lead to the combination of the only operators of non-stop services. On the Frankfurt–Pittsburgh, Frankfurt–Charlotte and Munich–Philadelphia routes, the operation would lead to the combination of the only operator of non-stop services (U.S. Air) with the largest or second-largest provider of competitive indirect flights.

In addition, the investigation showed that the congestion at Frankfurt and Munich airports constituted a substantial barrier to entry and expansion on these routes, because airlines seeking to provide new or additional services would have difficulties in obtaining the required slots to operate flights.

The parties proposed undertakings to overcome the Commission's concerns. United committed itself to making slots available at Frankfurt and Munich airports for new air service providers or existing providers commencing certain new or additional competitive air service, namely a non-stop or indirect scheduled passenger air service operated on a daily basis (or no less than six times a week) on one or more of the four identified city-pairs, if the providers in question are unable to obtain the slots through normal procedures. However, United is not required to make slots available with respect to an identified city-pair (i) once a carrier has commenced a new or additional competitive air service on that route, or (ii) when neither United nor any of its alliance partners offers a non-stop service on any of the identified city-pairs.

Degussa/Laporte

On March 12, the Commission cleared Degussa's acquisition of sole control of Laporte. Both companies are active in the manufacturing of specialty and other chemical products.

The Commission's investigation focused on the product markets concerning persulfates, cationic reagents and hydroxy monomers, in which the parties had substantial overlaps. In these markets, defined as EEA-wide with the exception of one cationic reagent for which the Commission looked at a worldwide market, the parties' combined market shares exceeded 70%, 50% and 60%, respectively. With respect to persulfates, the parties were the only European manufacturers.

The parties offered commitments to eliminate the Commission's concerns, including the divestiture of Degussa's persulfate plant, Laporte's plant producing all of its cationic reagents and other chemicals, and Laporte's plant that includes its entire monomers business.

The divestiture of Laporte's plants would also affect Laporte's activities other than those that related to the markets concerned and for which the Commission did not identify any competition concerns. However, the Commission considered it necessary to divest all these assets in order to offer a viable business to a potential acquiror and to create an effective competitor in the cationic reagents and hydroxy monomers markets.

Seagram/Pernod Ricard/Diageo

On May 8, the Commission approved the acquisition of Seagram's spirits and wine business by Pernod Ricard and Diageo, subject to conditions. Seagram belongs to the Vivendi Universal group and is active in spirits and wines on a worldwide basis. Both Ricard Pernod and Diageo[61] are active in the manufacture and supply of spirits worldwide.

The Commission examined the spirits sector and confirmed its narrow market definition, distinguishing between individual spirit categories, such as whiskey, rum, gin, vodka, tequila and flavored spirits. The Commission considered the relevant geographic market to be national.

The Commission's investigation focused on two main areas of concern: (i) in Iceland, the proposed transaction would add Captain Morgan, a locally dominant rum brand, to Diageo's already strong position there, and (ii) the addition of Four Roses, a bourbon whiskey, to either Pernod Ricard's or Diageo's portfolio could raise problems in a number of national markets.

To alleviate the Commission's concerns, the parties proposed separating the distribution of the Captain Morgan brand from that of other Diageo brands in Iceland, and selling Four Roses to a third party.

Nestlé/Ralston Purina

On July 27, the Commission approved Nestlé's acquisition of Ralston Purina.

The parties agreed to divest certain businesses as going concerns to alleviate concerns arising from overlaps between the parties' activities in Greece, Italy and Spain. Interestingly, the divestiture was not accompanied by an assignment to the purchaser of the brands used for the divested products, but rather by an exclusive brand license for three years from the divestiture, followed by an almost five-year period during which the parties could not use the brands in question in those countries. The Commission considered that this almost eight-year period overall would allow the purchaser to re-brand the products successfully. At the same time, licensing the brands, rather than assigning them, would, according to the Commission, avoid a permanent split in the ownership of the pet food brands in questions among different companies in different parts of the Community.

In Italy and Greece, where the parties do not have production facilities, the Commission accepted a commitment to transfer to the purchaser the existing commercial relationships between the divested businesses and their respective distributors and customers, and to supply the purchaser with the relevant products at cost during the period of the brand license.

---

61 Diageo was created through the merger between Grand Metropolitan plc and Guiness plc in 1997, see Case IV/M.938 *Guiness/Grand Metropolitan* OJ 1998 L 288/24.

3.6. FIRST-PHASE DECISION WITHOUT UNDERTAKINGS

Philips/Marconi Medical Systems

On October 17, the Commission cleared the acquisition by Koninklijke Philips Electronics N.V. (Philips) of the radiology imaging equipment and medical imaging equipment businesses of Marconi Medical Systems (MMS).

The new entity acquired a leading position, or strengthened Philips's leading position, in several EU countries. Nevertheless, the Commission found that the transaction did not eliminate Philips's closest competitor (as evidenced by the results of tenders issued in 2000-2001) and considered that the low switching costs faced by customers, the bidding nature of the market, reduced hospital budgets, the countervailing buying power of hospitals and the importance of technological innovation would have a disciplinary effect on product prices.

The Commission also considered that these market characteristics would exclude collective dominance or the coordination of commercial behavior by the three leading players (Siemens, GE and Philips Medical Systems), which together account for almost 100% of the magnetic resonance and nuclear medicine markets and around 85% of the computed tomography market in the EEA. In addition, the Commission expected other global players, in particular Hitachi or Toshiba, to expand their presence in these markets if the three leading firms were to raise their prices.

4. JOINT VENTURES

Smith & Nephew/Beiersdorf

On January 30, the Commission authorized a joint venture between Smith & Nephew plc and Beiersdorf AG subject to a package of divestitures.[62]

The joint venture combines the activities of the medical products companies with regard to sales of a variety of wound care, bandaging and phlebology products to professional users, such as hospitals. The Commission found that the joint venture would have created significant overlaps with regard to a number of products in seven Member States. The Commission reached its findings by defining the relevant markets nationally with regard to individual medical products. It stated that although Directive 93/42 on medical devices has been fully implemented, there are still indications that national product specifications, different traditions and habits of medical practitioners play a role in relation to some products. To remedy the Commission's concerns, the parties agreed to divest certain businesses, including goodwill, customer contacts, technical know-how and other intellectual property rights, as well as personnel and certain manufacturing equipment. In addition, any purchaser of the divested businesses needed to be approved by the Commission.

The Post Office/TNT/Singapore Post

On March 14, the Commission authorized the creation of two joint ventures between the national public postal operators of the United Kingdom, the Netherlands and Singapore subject to the divestiture by TNT Group (the Dutch operator) of its international mail division.[63]

The two joint ventures will together have a worldwide presence and be active in the provision of outbound cross-border business mail services and, to a limited extent, outbound cross-border parcel services. The Commission opened an in-depth

---

[62] Commission Press Release IP/01/126 January 31, 2001.
[63] Commission Press Release IP/01/364 March 14, 2001.

Part I: EC Competition Developments

investigation on November 15, 2000, because it identified possible competition problems arising from the parties' existing operations in the Netherlands and the United Kingdom. More specifically, the Commission was concerned by the elimination of competition between one of the joint ventures' businesses and its Dutch and U.K. parent companies.

The Phase II investigation confirmed the Commission's concerns about the market for outbound cross-border business mail in the Netherlands, though not concerns about the U.K. market.

The creation of the joint ventures would have eliminated competition between the Dutch incumbent and the most successful entrant into the Dutch market, The Post Office. The parties agreed to divest TNT's international mail division, the business unit that was originally intended to be contributed to one of the joint ventures. The parties proposed an up-front buyer solution, agreeing not to complete the transaction until the conclusion of a definitive purchase agreement with a purchaser approved by the Commission.

T-Online/TUI/C&N

On June 5, T-Online, TUI and C&N (Neckermann) withdrew their notification of a new online travel agency joint venture. The withdrawal came after it became apparent that the Commission's market investigation would conclude that the new venture could dominate the online travel market, foreclose other online suppliers and lead to the creation or strengthening of a dominant position on the overall travel agency market.

The joint venture was intended to be an online travel agency offering various products to end-consumers in Germany (*e.g.*, leisure package trips, last-minute vacations, flights, hotel rooms) by using the services of T-Online, a Deutsche Telekom subsidiary and Germany's leading supplier of internet-access services operating one of the most popular internet portals in Germany. TUI, a subsidiary of Preussag AG, and C&N (Neckermann), jointly owned by Lufthansa AG and Karstadt Quelle AG, would have made product offerings online via the joint venture. On May 8, the Commission opened a second-phase investigation into the planned joint venture, mainly because its preliminary investigation identified the provision of online travel services as the relevant product market.[64] According to the Commission, this market is distinct from the provision of services by

---

[64] Commission Press Release IP/01/670 May 8, 2001.

traditional travel agencies because online customers can search and book trips anytime, regardless of shopping hours and without leaving home. In addition, suppliers of online travel services face lower distribution costs.

This narrow market definition, however, is in sharp contrast to past Commission findings and probably marks a departure in this sector. In past decisions, the Commission viewed the services provided by virtual travel agencies as being substitutable with services provided by traditional travel agencies.[65] However, the Commission did not previously exclude the possibility that two distinct markets (online and traditional) could be identified as a result of an independent evolution of the online travel agency sector.

In the Commission's view, the joint venture could have privileged access to package holiday products through the two leading German tour operators and to a very large potential customer base through T-Online. Also, it appeared that other online travel agencies were dependent on the product offerings of the two leading German tour operators to a large extent. During the investigation, to competing online agencies voiced their concerns that the new online agency could have discriminated against them in the award of agency contracts.

IBM Italia/Business Solutions

On July 2, the Commission authorized a joint venture between IBM Italia and Business Solutions, an information technology (IT) services subsidiary of Italian automaker FIAT. The parties formed the joint venture as part of an outsourcing strategy, under which FIAT established a strategic partnership with IBM to rationalize its spending in the IT sector and IBM expanded its activities in the provision of IT services. The joint venture created one single economic entity comprising three separate legal entities: one entity acts as the marketing and distribution organization for the other two, which provide IT services. These two latter entities were contractually obliged to sell their services through the marketing entity. Despite the joint venture's legal structure, the Commission considered its creation as a single concentration because all three entities involved are highly interdependent and will act and appear in the market as one business.

Concerning the issue of joint control, the Commission concluded that the parties have *de facto* joint control over the joint venture. The Commission could not assume that the parties are able to exercise *de jure* joint control, because the three

---

[65] COMP/M.2197 *Hilton/Accor/Forte/Travel Services JV* February 16, 2001.

Part I: EC Competition Developments

separate entities' governance is set forth in separate agreements with slightly different rules: while IBM appoints the majority of the Boards of Directors of the two entities providing IT services, FIAT appoints the majority of the Board of Directors of the entity acting as marketing organization. However, the Commission concluded that the voting requirements set forth in the company agreements lead to *de facto* joint control because both parties share a common interest in cooperating fully and jointly exercising decisive influence.[66] This was because the activities of the three legal entities were highly interdependent and integrated within the joint venture's binding work-sharing agreements.

Covisint

On July 31, the Commission cleared the creation of Covisint, an internet marketplace for the automotive industry. Covisint was reviewed under Article 81 since the partners do not, within the meaning of the EC Merger Regulation, jointly control it.[67]

The Commission stressed that B2B marketplaces usually have pro-competitive effects as they create more market transparency and efficiencies ultimately resulting in lower prices for consumers. However, the Commission emphasized that these pro-competitive effects may be outweighed by negative effects, such as discrimination against certain classes of users leading ultimately to foreclosure, the exchange of, or access to, market-sensitive information by users of the marketplace, or joint selling or purchasing falling within the scope of Article 81(1).

The Commission concluded that the underlying contractual arrangements sufficiently take account of these concerns because Covisint is open to all firms, does not discriminate between shareholders and non-equity participants, provides for adequate data protection, including firewalls and security rules, and does not allow joint purchasing among users.

Hutchinson/NTT DoCoMo/KPN Mobile

On September 5, the Commission authorized a joint venture between Hutchison Whampoa, NTT DoCoMo, and KPN Mobile. The new joint venture was awarded

---

[66] The Commission's conclusion essentially confirms its similar findings on the issue of *de facto* joint control in Case IV/M.072 *Sanofi/Sterling Drug* June 10, 1991.

[67] Commission Press Release IP/01/1155 July 31, 2001.

4. Joint Ventures

one of the five third-generation mobile phone licenses in the United Kingdom, where it will build and operate a Universal Mobile Telephony Service (UMTS) network.

The Commission found that the parties do not *de jure* jointly control the joint venture, because major decisions are made by a simple majority. *De facto* joint control was nevertheless found to exist because the parents have veto rights over strategic decisions concerning the joint venture's business policy, including decisions with major investment implications and the appointment of senior management. Also, the Commission found that the parents would likely carry out a common policy because the joint venture was part of a strategic cooperation under which each parent contributed a vital component to the joint venture: Hutchison paid for the UMTS license, NTT DoCoMo was to provide the necessary mobile internet access technology and KPN Mobile had the knowledge of the European mobile phone markets required for the venture's success.[68]

The Commission's decision is in line with its past findings, particularly in *Symbian II*,[69] where it found that the parents did not jointly control the venture. In that case, the Commission could not establish that each of the four parent companies made a vital contribution to the venture. The Commission also found that the parents would not necessarily always vote together on strategic matters and that their interests in the venture's operation could diverge, depending upon the evolution of their respective positions as potential competitors in the downstream market for wireless information devices.

Hitachi/LG Electronics

On September 14, the Commission authorized a global joint venture between Hitachi and LG Electronics for the development, design and marketing of optical data-storage disk drives, including CD- and DVD-drives for computers. Production of the drives was to be out-sourced to the parents or to independent electronic manufacturers and marketed under an independent brand not referring to either parent. The Commission nevertheless considered the joint venture fully functional

---

[68] The Commission referred in this connection to ¶ 34 of its Notice on the Concept of Concentration, which explains that *de facto* control may be found more easily if the parents make vital contributions to the joint venture (OJ 1998 C 66/5).

[69] Case COMP/JV.12 *Ericsson/Nokia/Psion/Motorola* December 22, 1998, p. 3.

Part I: EC Competition Developments

because the out-sourcing of manufacturing was, according to the Commission, not unusual in high-tech industries, in particular in the computers and telecommunications area.[70]

BP Chemicals/Solvay

On October 29, the Commission authorized a joint venture between BP Chemicals and Solvay, combining BP Chemicals's High Density Polyethylene (HDPE) resin production and marketing business in Europe with Solvay's HDPE resin production, technology, research and marketing businesses in Europe and the United States.[71]

The Commission found the joint venture fully functional, although it was to be supplied by its parents with a significant proportion of its total ethylene requirements in Europe for the first years of its existence. The Commission found that the joint venture would not be dependent upon its parents to an extent that would jeopardize its ability to conduct its business independently. First, the supply arrangements between the joint venture and its parents simply mirrored the integrated nature of the joint venture's competitors, as all other HDPE producers were also vertically integrated. Second, the supply agreements' duration reflected general industry practice. Third, the joint venture would add significant value to the raw material (for some HDPE resin grades, as high as 59%). The Commission also considered that certain put/call options in the joint venture agreement do not undermine the joint venture's long-term nature.[72]

---

[70] See, *e.g.*, Case COMP/M.2394 *SCI/Nokia Networks* April 25, 2001.

[71] The formation of the joint venture was part of a series of transactions restructuring BP's polymer business and Solvay's polypropylene business.

[72] In this connection, the Commission refers to its similar findings in Case IV/M.722 *Teneo/Merrill Lynch/Bankers Trust* April 15, 1996, p. 2.

5. STATE AID

5.1. ECJ – JUDGMENTS

Case C-99/98 Austria v Commission

On February 15, the Court of Justice annulled a decision of the Commission to initiate a formal investigation procedure under Article 93(2) EC of Austrian state aid to Siemens.[73]

The Austrian government had notified the intended aid to the Commission in June 1996. After a lengthy exchange of correspondence, the Commission decided in February 1998 to open a formal investigation procedure. The Austrian government objected because the Commission had taken too long to reach its decision. The Court upheld the appeal of the Austrian government.

The Court had previously observed that the Commission is required to keep the preliminary phase between the notification of new aid and the opening of a formal procedure to a reasonable period of no more than two months.[74] The preliminary phase is intended only to allow the Commission to form a *prima facie* opinion of the compatibility of the aid with the Treaty. If the Commission fails to respect this time limit, the Member State can put into effect the notified aid, provided it has given the Commission prior notice of its intention to do so. The examination of the aid will then fall under the procedures governing existing aid.

The Court found that the Austrian government's notification must be considered to have been completed at the latest in March 1997, since the Commission had all the necessary information to form a *prima facie* opinion on the notified aid as from that date. The Commission therefore had exceeded the two-month period.

The Court also rejected the Commission's claim that the two-month period was not a strict deadline but could be prolonged in complex cases. The Court observed

---

[73] 2001 ECR I-1101.

[74] Case 120/73 *Lorenz* 1973 ECR 1471; Case 121/73 *Markmann* 1973 ECR 1495; Case 122/73 *Nordsee* 1973 ECR 1511; Case 141/73 *Lohrey* 1973 ECR 1527.

that the two-month period was set to safeguard the principle of legal certainty and that this objective would be jeopardized if the time limit were not binding.

Case C-379/98 PreussenElektra v Schlesswag

On March 13, the Court of Justice rendered its judgment concerning a German statute that requires regional electricity distributors to purchase, at fixed minimum prices, electricity produced from renewable energy sources within their area of supply.[75] The statute also obliges upstream suppliers of conventional-source electricity partially to compensate the regional distributors for their additional costs in doing so.

One of the central questions in the case was whether the notion of state aid requires the transfer of state resources or whether the rules on state aid also apply to state measures that transfer resources from one private undertaking to another, as in the present case.

Advocate General Jacobs stated that financing through state resources is a necessary element of the concept of state aid[76] and the Court confirmed this view. The Court acknowledged that the purchase obligation imposed by the German statute conferred an economic advantage to producers of electricity from renewable sources. However, the Court held that only advantages granted directly or indirectly through state resources constituted state aid within the meaning of Article 87(1) EC. Because the obligation to purchase electricity produced from renewable sources at fixed minimum prices did not involve a direct or indirect transfer of state resources, the Court concluded that neither the obligation nor the allocation of its cost between electricity suppliers and network operators could be regarded as part of a system of state aid.

The Court's past case law on the requirement of a transfer of state resources has been somewhat ambiguous. The Court held in *Van Tiggele* that the fixing of minimum prices in favor of certain distributors did not constitute state aid because it did not entail the transfer of state resources.[77] In *Commission v France* and subsequently in *Greece v Commission*, on the other hand, the Court noted that the concept of state aid did not necessarily require the financing through state

---

[75] 2001 ECR I-2009.

[76] Opinion of Advocate General Jacobs of October 26, 2000, 2001 ECR I-2009.

[77] Case 82/77 1978 ECR 25.

resources.[78] In *Sloman Neptun* the Court seemed to return to its original case law, stating that only advantages that are granted directly or indirectly through state resources constitute state aid.[79] This finding was confirmed in several subsequent judgments.[80]

In *PreussenElektra*, the Court also rejected the Commission's claim that the prohibition contained in Article 10 EC against jeopardizing the objectives of the EC Treaty requires that support measures determined by the state, but financed by private undertakings, be considered state aid.[81]

It is likely that the Court was motivated by a desire to prevent an overbroad application of state aid rules. As Advocate General Jacobs observed in his opinion, an extensive interpretation of the concept of state aid would create considerable legal uncertainty, as all national legislation regulating relations between private undertakings would have to be examined on the question whether it constituted state aid.

On the other hand, a concept of state aid limited to the transfer of state resources enables circumvention of state aid rules and creates inequalities that seem difficult to justify. As *PreussenElektra* illustrates, the same effect can be achieved either through state subsidies or through the direct transfer of financial resources between private undertakings. Arguably, where the payor and beneficiary are competitors, a state-imposed transfer of resources between private undertakings will even have more serious effects on competition than state subsidies.

The Court seems to assume that, in the case of mandated direct transfers, competition will be safeguarded by the affected undertakings, which are likely to contest such measures under national law.

---

[78] Case 290/83 1985 ECR 439 and Case 57/86 1988 ECR 2855. See also Case 173/73 *Italy v Commission* 1974 ECR 709, where the Court of Justice observed that funds financed through compulsory contributions imposed by state legislation (and managed and apportioned in accordance with that legislation) must be regarded as state resources, even if they are administered by institutions distinct from the public authorities.

[79] Joined Cases C-72/91 and C-73/91 1993 ECR I-887.

[80] Case C-189/91 *Kirsammer-Hack* 1993 ECR I-6185; Joined Cases C-52/97, C-53/97 and C-54/97 *Viscido* 1998 ECR I-2629; Case C-200/97 *Ecotrade* 1998 ECR I-7907; Case C-295/97 *Piaggio* 1999 ECR I-3735.

[81] C-379/98 2000 ECR I-2099.

Part I: EC Competition Developments

Case C-204/97 Portuguese Republic v Commission

On May 3, the Court of Justice rendered its judgment in a case concerning French aid granted to producers of liqueur wines,[82] which are more heavily taxed than producers of naturally sweet wines. Following a tax strike by French liqueur wine producers, the French government adopted an aid plan in their favor. The aid was approved by the Commission under Article 88(3) EC without opening a formal procedure. The Court annulled this decision in an action brought by the Portuguese Republic.

The Court recalled that the Commission, when examining the legality of aid, can restrict itself to the preliminary phase under Article 88(3) only in cases that create no serious difficulties. On the other hand, where the Commission cannot overcome all difficulties raised by a case in the preliminary phase, it must open a formal investigation procedure under Article 88(2).

The Court noted that there was strong evidence that the aid in question was intended to compensate French liqueur wine producers for the higher level of tax imposed on liqueur wine. This might result in a situation where only liqueur wine producers from other Member States would have to bear the economic weight of the higher tax. As a consequence, the aid scheme might infringe the prohibition of discriminatory taxation under Article 90.

The Court pointed out that state aid that infringes other provisions of the EC Treaty cannot be approved by the Commission. The Court considered that the link between the system of taxation and the aid plan represented a serious difficulty in determining whether the aid plan was compatible with the EC Treaty. The Commission was thus required to examine in a formal investigation under Article 92(2) whether this link constituted an infringement of Article 90 and consequently whether the aid was compatible with the common market.

Case C-143/99 Adria-Wien Pipeline v Finanzlandesdirektion für Kärnten

This case arose out of the introduction by Austria in 1996 of a tax on the consumption of electricity and gas. The relevant legislation provides that undertakings, the main activity of which is the production of physical goods, can obtain a partial reimbursement of the tax. This rule has the effect of easing the burden of the new tax in the agricultural and manufacturing sectors, as only undertakings in the

---

[82] 2001 ECR I-3175.

service sector and private energy users have to bear the full tax. The essential question was therefore whether this different tax burden constitutes, in effect, a grant of state aid.

On May 8, Advocate General Mischo rendered his opinion, concluding that the advantage granted to the agricultural and manufacturing sectors is not of sufficiently selective nature to be treated as state aid.[83] According to the Advocate General, special rules applying to the entire primary and secondary industry sectors cannot be regarded as exceptions to a general system of taxation. Rather, the disputed tax should be seen as establishing a new general system of taxation that inherently includes the principle that the primary and secondary industry sectors should not be taxed on the basis of their full energy consumption.

As a subsidiary matter, the Advocate General also raised the question whether tax advantages granted with respect to a newly introduced tax can be said to be financed by state resources, as required by Article 81(1). According to the Advocate General, it would be possible to argue that the state does not give up a claim to tax revenue with regard to such advantages because the state did not have a claim to tax revenue from the agricultural and manufacturing sectors before the introduction of the new tax system. As a consequence, the advantage could not be said to be financed by state resources within the meaning of the case law of the Court of Justice. The Advocate General ultimately left the question open, in view of his conclusions regarding the selective nature of the tax system.

On November 8, the Court of Justice rendered a preliminary ruling in the matter. The Court rejected the Advocate General's suggestion that tax advantages granted with respect to new taxes could not be viewed as being financed by state resources, holding that it was irrelevant whether the beneficiary of the tax advantage was better or worse off in comparison with the situation under the old tax regime. This is consistent with the *Ferring* case, which similarly concerned an advantage resulting from the non-imposition of a new tax, and in which Advocate General Tizzano took the view that such an advantage was financed by state resources because the state in effect renounced the possibility of collecting the tax from the exempted undertakings.[84]

The Court then turned to the question whether the tax advantage at issue was of a selective or a general nature. Again contrary to Advocate General Mischo's view, the Court held that neither the large number of undertakings benefiting from the

---

[83] 2001 ECR I-8365.

[84] Opinion of Advocate General Tizzano of May 8, 2001, 2001 ECR I-9067.

provision nor the diversity and size of the industry to which those undertakings belong precludes the existence of state aid. Rather, according to the Court, tax rebates will constitute state aid if the criteria for granting them are not justified by the nature or general scheme of the national tax legislation.

In this case, Austria argued that the limitation of the rebates to manufacturing companies was justified because the energy tax weighed more heavily on those industries. The Court did not share this view, pointing out that companies active in the service sector may be major energy consumers just like manufacturing companies. Accordingly, the limitation of the tax rebates could not be justified by the general scheme of the Austrian tax system. As a result, the Court held that the limitation of the tax rebates to manufacturing companies constituted state aid.

It is interesting to compare this judgment with Advocate General Tizzano's opinion in *Ferring*, in which he suggested that a tax exemption should constitute state aid only if the beneficiaries and the excluded companies are competitors.[85] Arguably, the test proposed in *Ferring* is narrower and more precise than the test applied in *Adria-Wien Pipeline*. The Court's test leaves more discretion to decide whether selective tax advantages constitute state aid, though it seems questionable whether selective tax advantages should fall under EC state aid law in the absence of a competitive relationship between the beneficiaries and the excluded companies.

Case C-53/00 Ferring v Agence Centrale des Organismes de Sécurité Sociale

This matter concerned a French tax imposed on direct sales by pharmaceutical producers. In France, pharmaceutical wholesalers must maintain sufficient stocks to guarantee the supply of pharmacies in their sector. By contrast, pharmaceutical producers selling directly to pharmacies are not subject to this obligation. In 1997, a special tax was introduced in France, which was levied only on direct sales of pharmaceutical producers to pharmacies. The tax was designed to compensate pharmaceutical wholesalers for the competitive disadvantage that they suffered *vis-à-vis* pharmaceutical producers because of their public service obligation. Ferring SA, a pharmaceutical producer, brought an action against this tax in a national court. It argued that the exemption of wholesalers from the tax constituted illegal state aid. The court referred the case for a preliminary ruling to the Court of Justice.

---

[85] *Ibid.*

On May 8, Advocate General Tizzano rendered his opinion.[86] First, the Advocate General examined whether the tax exemption is state aid. The central question in this regard is whether the non-imposition of a new tax on certain categories of companies could be viewed as the grant of a selective advantage in their favor.

The Advocate General pointed out that treating the imposition of taxes on a limited category of companies as aid in favor of exempted categories could be an over broad application of state aid rules. Excluding *a priori* such tax schemes from the rules, on the other hand, would allow Member States to circumvent these rules easily. According to the Advocate General, the question therefore requires a case-by-case analysis taking into account the specific competitive relationship between the taxed and exempted companies.

Though the new tax was explicitly intended to readjust the competitive balance between pharmaceutical producers and wholesalers, the Advocate General found that the tax scheme was not state aid. In the present case, the exemption from the disputed tax was intended to compensate the wholesalers for the costs of the public service of maintaining the required stocks. According to the Advocate General, compensation for public service does not constitute state aid, provided that the compensation does not exceed the costs of the service. The Advocate General rejected the rulings of the Court of First Instance in *FFSA*[87] and *SIC*,[88] which treated such compensation as state aid and argued that, taken together, the public service obligation and the compensation are economically neutral and are therefore not properly characterized as "aid."

As a subsidiary matter, the Advocate General examined whether the disputed tax system could be declared compatible with the EC Treaty if the Court of Justice were nevertheless to treat the tax system as state aid. In such an event, the Advocate General concluded that the measure would be justified under the public service exception of Article 86(2) EC insofar as the compensation represented by the tax system does not exceed the costs of the public service provided by the pharmaceutical wholesalers and is necessary for the provision of that service.

However, if the disputed tax system were treated as containing an element of state aid, the question would arise whether the failure of France to notify to the Commission such new aid renders the system void. The Advocate General

---

[86] *Ibid.*

[87] Case T-106/95 1997 ECR II-229.

[88] Case T-46/97 2000 ECR II-2125.

concluded that there is no need for Commission approval under Article 87 because the system is justified under Article 86(2), a directly applicable provision that can be applied by the national judge. According to the Advocate General, the formal failure to notify the disputed tax system should not lead to its invalidity, even if it were regarded as containing an element of state aid.

On November 22, the Court of Justice rendered a preliminary ruling in the matter, substantially agreeing with the Advocate General. The Court held that the exemption of wholesalers from the tax gave them an economic advantage granted by the State because the State had waived its right to receive the corresponding tax payments. However, recalling that the exemption is designed to offset the costs borne by wholesalers resulting from the maintenance of minimum stocks in the public interest, the Court held that the exemption could be viewed as a compensation for the public service provided by the wholesalers, and concluded that the exemption would not constitute state aid if it corresponded to the costs incurred by the wholesalers. The Court left it to the national court to examine whether this was the case.

This judgment sheds new light on the rules governing compensation for public services. The Court has held in previous cases that state payments for the compensation of public services do not constitute state aid.[89] In *Ferring*, the Court goes a step further by recognizing that such compensation may also be made indirectly, not by payment to the undertaking rendering the public services, but by imposing additional financial burdens on competing undertakings that do not bear the costs of those services.

5.2. CFI – JUDGMENTS

Case T-156/98 RJB Mining v Commission

On January 31, the Court of First Instance annulled a Commission decision authorizing the merger between RAG and Saarbergwerke, two German coal producers.[90]

The transaction concerned the acquisition of the state-owned Saarbergwerke by RAG for the price of one Deutsche Mark. RJB Mining, a British coal producer had complained to the Commission about the transaction and brought an action against the Commission's approval before the Court.

---

[89] See Case 240/83 *ADBHU* 1985 ECR 531.
[90] 2001 ECR II-337.

The Court annulled the Commission's decision on the ground that the Commission had failed to assess the extent to which the possible state aid strengthened the financial and commercial power of RAG. Although the judgment of the Court was made under the ECSC Treaty, the Court's reasoning is of a general nature and will thus also be of relevance under the EC Treaty.

The Commission had acknowledged that the price paid for Saarbergwerke might include unnotified state aid up to one billion Deutsche Marks. It decided, however, to carry out a separate investigation under state aid rules and not to examine the question in the merger procedure.

The Court held that the Commission must assess the entire transaction. Although the Commission does not have to decide on the legality of the alleged aid in a formal preliminary decision, the Commission must avoid potential inconsistencies arising from the implementation of the various provisions of Community law. The Court concluded that the Commission could not, in its assessment of the transaction, refrain from examining whether and, if so, to what extent the financial and commercial power of the merged entity was strengthened by the alleged aid.

Case T-288/97 Regione Autonoma Friuli-Venezia Giulia v Commission

On April 4, the Court of First Instance rendered its judgment in an action for annulment brought by the Friuli-Venezia Giulia region against a Commission decision declaring aid granted to road transport undertakings established in the region incompatible with the EC Treaty.[91] The Court had already decided claims against the same decisions brought by the road transport undertakings in question.[92]

The Court observed that even aid of a relatively small amount is liable to affect trade between Member States if there is strong competition in the sector in which the recipient operates. According to the Court, this is particularly true where, as in the present case, the market is characterized by a large number of small-scale undertakings.

The Court stated that trade between Member States can also be affected even if recipient undertakings do not export goods or services, as the aid may create disadvantages for undertakings from other Member States that export to the Member State granting the aid.

---

[91] 2001 ECR II-1169.
[92] Joined Cases T-298/97, T-312/97, T-313/97, T-315/97, T-600/97 to T-607/97, T-1/98, T-3/98 to T-6/89, T-23/98 *Alzetta and Others v Commission* 2000 ECR II-2319.

A final point was that the transport sector was fully liberalized only after the relevant aid was granted. The applicant argued that this should prevent the aid in question from being treated as new aid under Article 87(1) EC. The Court agreed in principle that Article 87(1) applies only to sectors that are open to Community competition, and that aid granted in a market that was initially closed to competition must be treated as permissible existing aid when that market is liberalized.

However, in the present case, the Court distinguished between the international transport sector and the cabotage (domestic) sector. With regard to international road transport, the Court observed that Regulation 1018/69 had opened this sector to competition in 1969. Therefore, the aid granted to companies engaged in international road transport was correctly classified as new aid to which any incompatibility decision would apply.

6. POLICY AND PROCEDURE

6.1. CFI – JUDGMENTS

Case T-112/98 Mannesmannröhren-Werke AG v Commission

On February 20, in an action for annulment of a Commission decision requiring a party to respond to certain questions in the course of an Article 81 EC investigation, the Court of First Instance, in accordance with the Court of Justice's judgment in *Orkem v Commission*,[93] held that recipients of requests for information pursuant to Article 11 of Council Regulation 17 may limit themselves to answering questions of a purely factual nature and to producing only pre-existing documents and materials sought.[94] The Commission is not entitled to ask about the intention, aim or purpose of a particular practice or measure, where responding to such questions may compel a recipient to admit an infringement. These principles apply from the very first stage of an investigation initiated by the Commission.

For purposes of ensuring the efficacy of an Article 11 request, however, the Commission is entitled to require a company to provide all necessary information concerning facts known to it and to disclose any documents in its possession, even if these may be used to establish the existence of its anti-competitive conduct. To acknowledge an absolute right of silence would exceed what was necessary to preserve a company's rights of defense and would represent an unjustified obstacle to the Commission's performance of its duties.

The judgment arguably fails to consider recent developments before the European Court of Human Rights. At the time *Orkem* was decided, it had not been necessary for the European Court of Human Rights to decide whether Article 6 of the European Convention on Human Rights (the ECHR), dealing with the right against self-incrimination, contained a right to silence. However, in subsequent cases the European Court of Human Rights held that Article 6 does contain such a

---

[93] Case 374/87 1989 ECR 3283.
[94] 2001 ECR II-729.

right.[95] Some commentators argue that, because Community institutions should define fundamental rights under EU law taking into account the ECHR as interpreted by the European Court of Human Rights – including the right against self-incrimination as defined in *Funke* and *Saunders* – the Community Courts should overrule the *Orkem* principle and recognize a right to silence in EU competition investigations. In *Mannesmannröhren-Werke*, however, the Court of First Instance held that it had no jurisdiction to apply the ECHR when reviewing an investigation under competition law, inasmuch as the ECHR is not part of Community law. This may not be the final word, since Community courts do recognize fundamental principles of rights of defense and right to fair legal process, which is evident from the rights afforded to recipients of Article 11 requests.

Cases T-202/98, T-204/98 and T-207/98 Tate & Lyle, British Sugar and Napier Brown v Commission

On July 12, the Court of First Instance ruled on an appeal against the Commission's decision of October 1998 imposing fines of € 39.6 million on British Sugar, € 7 million on Tate and Lyle and € 1.8 million on Napier Brown.[96] The fines were imposed for meetings attended by these companies between 1986 and 1990 at which British Sugar provided information about its future prices for industrial and retail sugar. The companies contested the substance of the Commission's decision, but of particular interest is Tate & Lyle's challenge to the level of its fine and the Court's application of the Leniency Notice.

The Commission granted Tate & Lyle a 50% reduction in its fine in light of its cooperation in the investigation. Tate & Lyle argued, however, that its cooperation came within Section B of the Leniency Notice, thereby entitling it to a reduction of at least 75%. Tate & Lyle had submitted two self-incriminating letters to the Commission providing decisive evidence of the cartel's existence and enabling the Commission to intervene in the case. According to the Court, whether Tate & Lyle's cooperation came within Section B turned on whether its cooperation was continuous and complete within the meaning of Point B(d).

The Commission had not regarded Tate & Lyle's cooperation as continuous and complete because of two alleged retractions. First, while Tate & Lyle had

---

[95] Case 82/1991/334/407 *Funke* Series A no. 256A and Case 43/1994/490/572 *Saunders v United Kingdom*.
[96] 2001 ECR II-2035.

allegedly originally admitted an exchange of information between British Sugar and Tate & Lyle concerning discounts granted to certain customers, it later denied such exchange. The Commission asserted that it could not prove this element of the infringement because of Tate & Lyle's retraction. The Court nevertheless held that it was not for the Commission to find that Tate & Lyle was not cooperative in relation to an element of an infringement whose actual existence had not been established.

Furthermore, while at first Tate & Lyle had allegedly accepted that it had entered into an arrangement with British Sugar that infringed Article 81(1) EC, it later stated that such an arrangement was unnecessary as it was in any event obliged to follow the pricing policy of British Sugar (as a result of the effect of the Community sugar market scheme in Britain)[97] or, in other words, that it had not entered into any arrangement which breached Article 81(1). The Court found that while Tate & Lyle reinterpreted the facts, it neither challenged facts previously admitted nor retracted its statement that the disputed meetings fell under Article 81(1).

Accordingly, the Court found that the Commission had erroneously characterized the cooperation of Tate & Lyle as not being continuous and complete. The Court, however, proceeded to grant only a 60% reduction because (i) although Tate & Lyle had not retracted its original statements, it had nevertheless partially altered the characterization of facts previously established, and (ii) Tate & Lyle played a significant role in the cartel.

As a result, there is now some uncertainty about the application of the current Leniency Notice and the extent to which companies may offer a different slant on the facts without jeopardizing a reduction in the level of their fines.

British Sugar's challenge of the Commission's increase of its fine by 40% based on the infringement's duration is also of interest. Such an increase was excessive, argued British Sugar, absent market effects. The Court confirmed that duration is one of the factors the Commission may legitimately take into account when determining the level of a fine. As to the 40% increase, the Court confirmed that the Commission has discretion in fixing fines and need not apply a precise mathematical formula. The Court also explicitly rejected British Sugar's arguments that the Commission can raise a fine by reference to the duration of the infringement only if and to the extent that there is a direct relation between the duration and the

---

[97] The entire British beet sugar quota under the Community sugar market scheme is allocated to British Sugar, which therefore dominates the sugar market in Britain.

serious harm caused to the Community objectives of competition rules and that such relation is excluded absent any effects of the infringement on the market.

Case T-112/99 Métropole Télévision (M6), Suez-Lyonnaise des Eaux, France Télécom and Télévision Française 1 SA (TF1) v Commission

On September 18, the Court of First Instance rejected the rule of reason theory in applying Article 81(1) EC, both with regard to the transaction in question and to the accompanying ancillary restrictions.[98] This represents a clear divergence from the practice of U.S. antitrust law, which recognizes a rule of reason encompassing those factors assessed under Article 81(3).

The applicants notified to the Commission agreements establishing Télévision par Satellite (TPS), a partnership to devise, develop and broadcast a range of pay-TV programs and services. They sought clearance not only with regard to the creation of TPS, but also for three clauses in the agreements that they regarded as ancillary to the operation: a non-competition clause; a clause granting TPS a right of first refusal and a right of final refusal concerning the production of special-interest channels and television services by its shareholders; and a clause providing that the general-interest channels were to be broadcast exclusively by TPS. While the Commission found no grounds for action pursuant to Article 81(1) with regard to the creation of TPS, it cleared the three clauses only for a period of three years.

The applicants argued in particular that the Commission had misapplied Article 81(1) by failing to apply the rule of reason to the exclusivity clause and the clause relating to special-interest channels. Under the rule of reason, the analysis under Article 81(1) would include weighing the pro- and anti-competitive effects of an agreement for purposes of determining whether it is prohibited; the practice would fall outside the scope of Article 81(1) if it had more positive than negative effects on competition on a given market. The applicants asserted that the Court of Justice had confirmed the existence of such a rule of reason in *Nungesser and Eisle v Commission* and *Coditel v Ciné-Vog Films*.[99] The Court in the present case found that, while there were certain judgments in which the European courts had favored a more flexible interpretation of Article 81(1), those judgments could not be inter-

---

[98] Judgment of September 18, 2001, not yet published.

[99] Case 258/78 1982 ECR I-2015 and Case 262/81 1982 ECR I-3381.

preted as establishing the existence of a rule of reason in Community competition law.

According to the Court, when applying Article 81(1), account should be taken of the actual conditions in which the agreement functions (particularly the economic context in which the relevant undertakings operate), the products and services covered by the agreement, and the actual structure of the market concerned. This approach ensures that Article 81(1) is not applied in the abstract and without distinction to all agreements whose effect is to restrict the freedom of action of one or more of the parties. Such an approach, however, does not entail weighing the pro- and anti-competitive effects of an agreement when determining whether Article 81(1) applies.

The Court also stated that, when determining whether an ancillary restriction is objectively necessary, it is not a question of analyzing whether, in light of the relevant market, the restriction is indispensable to the commercial success of the main operation, but whether, in the specific context of the main operation, the restriction is necessary to implement that operation. Where the duration or scope of the restriction exceed what is necessary in order to implement the operation, the restriction must be assessed separately under Article 81(3) EC.

Case T-171/99 Corus UK Ltd. v Commission

On October 10, the Court of First Instance accepted an application by Corus UK Ltd. seeking interest from the European Commission on € 12 million repaid to Corus in April 1999 following a March 1999 judgment by the Court reducing a fine of € 32 million imposed by the Commission on Corus in 1993, which it paid in June 1994, for antitrust violations in its iron and steel operations.[100] The Commission had rejected Corus's request for interest on that sum from June 1994 to April 1999.

The Court considered the merits of the appeal under Article 34 ECSC, which requires that the Commission take all necessary steps to comply with a Court judgment annulling a Commission decision and that the Commission ensure equitable redress for any harm suffered through the Commission's fault.

With respect to the Commission's fault, the Court held that the mere reversal of a decision is insufficient to establish fault. Fault has been found by the European Court of Justice in cases of "inexcusable mistakes," "grave neglect of the duties of

---

[100] Judgment of October 10, 2001, not yet published.

supervision," and obvious "lack of care." In considering whether fault exists, the Court must also have regard to the complexity of the situations regulated by the particular Community institution, the difficulties in applying legislation, and the discretion available under the applicable legislation. In light of the history of relations between the iron and steel industry and the Commission between 1970 and 1994, the complexity of the cartel in question, the variety and number of the infringements by the cartel members, the care taken by cartel members to conceal the cartel, and the discretion afforded to the Commission when fixing fines, the Court had little difficulty in rejecting this part of the applicant's argument.

Nevertheless, the Court concluded that the payment of arrears of interest on the principal amount of the repaid fine is a step necessary for the enforcement of the annulment decision, even absent any fault on the Commission's part. In the Court's view, a judgment of annulment eliminates the annulled measure from the legal system, requiring the defendant to take the necessary measures to reverse the effects of the invalidated measures. In the case of an act already executed, this includes restoring the applicant to the position it would have been in but for the invalidated act. In this instance, the principal step is for the Commission to repay the excess fine paid by Corus. The Court found that this obligation also applies to default interest, first because this is an essential component of the Commission's obligation to restore the applicant to its original position, and second because failure to pay the interest could result in the unjust enrichment of the Community. The Court specifically rejected the Commission's argument that the loss caused to Corus resulted from Corus's own actions, in that Corus could merely have provided a bank guarantee rather than paying the fine immediately.

With regard to the rate of interest, the Commission followed the laws of the Member States, finding that, in cases of unjust enrichment, the claimant is normally entitled to the lower of the two amounts corresponding to the enrichment and the loss. Further, where the injury consists of the loss of use of money over a period of time, the amount recoverable is generally calculated by reference to the statutory or judicial rate of interest. Corus was awarded a sum of just over € 3 million. Interestingly, since June 2000, when a company appeals a Commission decision imposing a fine and that company has already paid the fine, the Commission places the fine in an interest-bearing account opened for that purpose by the Commission.

6. Policy and Procedure

Cases T-45/98 and T-47/98 Krupp Thyssen Stainless GmbH and Acciai Speciali Terni SpA v Commission

On December 13, the Court of First Instance gave judgment in an appeal by Krupp Thyssen Stainless GmbH (KTN) and Acciai Speciali Terni SpA (AST) against the Commission's decision of January 1998 fining seven stainless steel manufacturers over € 70 million for cartel-related antitrust violations.[101]

The first interesting aspect of this case concerns the responsibility of one company for the antitrust violations of another company. In January 1995, KTN acquired Thyssen Stahl AG, which had also been engaged in anti-competitive behavior since 1993. KTN agreed at the date of acquisition to accept liability for any infringements committed by Thyssen Stahl. During the Commission investigation and in the statement of objections issued in April 1997, the Commission continued to treat KTN and Thyssen Stahl separately.

In July 1997, in response to a request by the Commission, KTN confirmed that it assumed liability for Thyssen Stahl's acts, including those dating back to 1993. It was accepted during the Court proceedings that, in view of this confirmation, the Commission could have been entitled to attribute to KTN liability for the unlawful pre-acquisition conduct of Thyssen Stahl, though in principle the natural or legal person running the undertaking at the time of the infringement would ordinarily be held accountable for it. However, the Court also found that, since KTN had accepted liability for Thyssen Stahl, KTN should have been given the right to be heard regarding the conduct attributed to Thyssen Stahl. Because the statement of objections relating to Thyssen Stahl's conduct had not been addressed to KTN and KTN had not been given the opportunity to submit comments, the Commission was not entitled to attribute liability to KTN for the acts of Thyssen Stahl.

The second point of interest in this case relates to the method of imposing fines on companies within the same corporate group. KTN, which also acquired the other applicant, AST, in May 1996, criticized the Commission for not taking into account the group relationship between KTN, AST and Thyssen Stahl when calculating the fines. In calculating the fines for all the infringers, the Commission did not have regard to the turnover of the companies, but fixed a base sum of € 4 million for each of the three of them. KTN argued that this approach was discriminatory, as three fines were imposed on a single economic entity. The Court, however, agreed with the Commission's argument that, since the three companies

---

[101] Judgment of December 13, 2001, not yet published.

acted independently on the market, the imposition of three separate fines was in accordance with established case-law.

The third point of interest in this case concerns the application of Section D of the Leniency Notice, which allows for a reduction in fines where information is provided that contributes to establishing the existence of an infringement before the Commission issues a statement of objections. The applicants claimed that, where several undertakings reply at or around the same time to questions from the Commission, disclosing facts that confirm the Commission's suspicions, the order in which undertakings provide the information does not justify treating them differently for purposes of reducing the fine. The Commission claimed that the applicants had not provided any new documentary evidence or facts not already in the Commission's possession, since another of the stainless steel producers, questioned by the Commission before the applicants, had already provided the relevant information. The Court found that the Commission must follow the principle of equal treatment when applying Section D and that the mere fact that one undertaking was the first to acknowledge the contested facts in response to Commission questions does not constitute an objective reason for treating them differently.

6.2. COMMISSION – DECISION

Amino Acids

On June 7, the Commission published its decision imposing fines totaling € 110 million on Archer Daniels Midland (ADM), Ajinomoto Inc., Kyowa Hakko Kogyo Ltd. (Kyowa), Sewon Europe GmbH (Sewon) and Cheil Jedang Corporation (Cheil) for agreements between June 1990 and June 1995 pursuant to which these lysine manufacturers fixed prices, controlled supply, allocated sales volumes and exchanged information on sales volumes.[102] The Commission found that the cartel represented a very serious infringement of EC competition rules in accordance with the guidelines on the method of setting fines pursuant to Article 15(2) of Regulation No. 17 and Article 65(5) of the ECSC Treaty.[103]

The companies involved produced synthetic lysine, an essential amino acid used by nutritionists to formulate protein diets tailored to the needs of livestock. This case is interesting not least because of the extent to which the companies

---

[102] OJ 2001 L 152/24.
[103] OJ 1998 C 9/3.

involved cooperated with the Commission before and during its investigation, and for the Commission's application of its Notice on the non-imposition or reduction of fines in cartel cases (the Leniency Notice).[104] The Commission granted four companies significant reductions in their fines under the Leniency Notice.

In July 1996, shortly before several of the companies involved in the Commission investigation were charged by the U.S. antitrust authorities with engaging in a conspiracy to suppress and eliminate competition by fixing the price and allocating sales volumes of lysine, Ajinomoto informed the Commission about the existence of the cartel covering the period from ADM's entry into the EEA lysine market in June 1992 to June 1995. In offering its full cooperation, Ajinomoto relied on the then-new Leniency Notice. Although Ajinomoto was the first company to come forward and provide decisive evidence of the cartel, the Commission did not find that Ajinomoto satisfied the conditions for full immunity from fines under the Leniency Notice since (i) Ajinomoto had not provided the Commission with all relevant information and therefore its cooperation with the Commission had not been complete, and (ii) Ajinomoto had been a leader in the infringement. Ajinomoto was nevertheless granted a 50% reduction in its fine.

Concerning the failure to disclose all information, the Commission noted that it is not for the company relying on the Leniency Notice to determine the scope of the subject of the Commission's investigation, and that Ajinomoto should have pointed to the information in question in order to have the Commission's guidance as to its relevance. As to Ajinomoto's being a leader of the cartel, while acknowledging that immunity for leaders (in cases where there is more than one leader) would provide an incentive for leaders to come forward first with decisive evidence of a cartel's existence, the Commission stated that the balance between granting favorable treatment to cooperative offenders and deterring future offenders would be disturbed if immunity was available to cartel members that played a determining role in the infringement.

Interestingly, under the Commission's new draft Leniency Notice (see below), immunity from fines is not lost merely because a company acted as an instigator or played a determining role in the illegal activity. A company must not, however, have coerced other undertakings, through its economic strength or otherwise, to participate in the illegal activity.

Sewon was also granted a 50% reduction in its fine because, although its cooperation with the Commission was not entirely voluntary, it was the first of the cartel members to provide complete decisive evidence concerning the infringe-

---

[104] OJ 1996 C 207/4.

ment, including for the period before ADM's entry into the EEA lysine market. Cheil and Kyowa were each granted reductions of 30% for providing evidence confirming the existence of the infringements. Although ADM did not cooperate with the Commission during the investigation, it received a reduction of 10% for not contesting the facts set forth in the Commission's statement of objections. Finally, the Commission made clear that companies may benefit from the Leniency Notice only with regard to self-incrimination and not with regard to "whistle blowing;" in other words, the Commission will reward only companies that would otherwise have been deterred from coming forward due to the risk of incurring fines.

6.3. COMMISSION – NOTICES

Draft Leniency Notice

On July 18, the Commission published a draft Leniency Notice[105] intended to replace the Leniency Notice adopted in 1996. The new Notice was designed to increase transparency and to clarify the conditions for reducing fines. There were two main aspects of the revision. First, complete immunity from fines would be granted to the first company to provide sufficient information to enable the Commission to launch a surprise inspection of a suspected cartel. (As ultimately adopted, the Notice clarifies that such immunity will be granted only if the Commission previously lacked sufficient evidence to commence such an investigation.) A company satisfying the conditions would promptly receive a letter from the Commission confirming immunity, provided it complied with the conditions set out in the Notice. Interestingly, under the new Notice, a company would not be disqualified from immunity merely because it acted as an instigator or played a determining role in the illegal activity – it must not, however, have coerced other undertakings to participate in the illegal activity. This represented a shift in the Commission's position in its previous Notice (and adopted in the lysine cartel case), and is similar to the U.S. antitrust practice of "zero dollars in fines" for companies that provide information leading to the detection of cartels.

The second main aspect of the new Notice was a modification in the policy on reduction of fines to allow the Commission, in addition to grants of full immunity,

---

[105] OJ 2001 C 205/18. The new Leniency Notice was ultimately adopted, with minimal substantive changes, in February 2002, OJ 2002 C 45/3.

to grant reductions to companies providing "added value" evidence to the Commission. The amount of any reduction would depend on the time at which evidence is provided and its quality. Companies eligible for a reduction would be informed of this preliminary conclusion by letter from the Commission no later than the date on which a statement of objections is notified.

General Application of the Leniency Notice

2001 witnessed 10 cartel decisions and fines on 56 companies totaling € 1.836 billion. In the "vitamins cartel,"[106] the Commission for the first time granted 100% immunity under the leniency notice to a company (Aventis SA), because it was the first to cooperate with the Commission and to provide decisive evidence in establishing the existence of anti-competitive conduct regarding two products. Subsequently, in the "carbonless paper cartel,"[107] the Commission also granted total immunity to Sappi Limited.

By contrast, in relation to the "citric acid cartel,"[108] Cerestar Bioproducts B.V. was granted only a 90% reduction since, although it was the first company to provide decisive evidence, it had approached the Commission only after it was fully aware that the cartel was the subject of an ongoing investigation by the Commission. Similarly, in the "sodium gluconate cartel,"[109] Fujisawa Pharmaceutical Company Ltd. received a reduction of only 80%, despite having supplied decisive evidence, as the company started to cooperate only after it received a request for information from the Commission.

De Minimis *Notice*

On December 22, the Commission replaced the existing *De Minimis* Notice, adopted in 1997, with a new Notice.[110]

The new Notice raises the *de minimis* market share threshold from 5% to 10% for agreements between actual or potential competitors and from 10% to 15%

---

[106] Commission Press Release IP/01/1625 November 21, 2001.

[107] Commission Press Release IP/01/1892 December 20, 2001.

[108] Commission Press Release IP/01/1743 December 5, 2001.

[109] Commission Press Release IP/01/1355 October 2, 2001.

[110] OJ 2001 C 368/13.

for agreements between non-competitors. The 10% threshold applies in cases of doubt.

The new Notice introduces a 5% *de minimis* threshold for agreements relating to markets where competition is restricted by the cumulative effects of parallel networks of similar agreements among several manufacturers or dealers (*e.g.*, in the beer and petrol sectors).

Concerning hard-core restrictions, *i.e.*, those restrictions that normally apply irrespective of the parties' market shares, the Notice follows the restrictions listed in Block Exemption Regulation 2658/2000 on specialization agreements for agreements between competitors[111] and in Block Exemption Regulation 2790/1999 on vertical agreements for agreements between non-competitors.[112]

The new Notice states that agreements between small- and medium-sized enterprises are in general *de minimis* and rarely capable of affecting trade between Member States.

The Commission will not institute proceedings, either upon application or on its own initiative, with respect to agreements covered by the new Notice, and will not impose fines where companies assume in good faith that an agreement is covered by the Notice.

---

[111] OJ 2000 L 304/3.

[112] OJ 1999 L 336/21.

PART II: NATIONAL COMPETITION DEVELOPMENTS

1. AUSTRIA

This section reviews developments concerning the Cartel Act of 1988, which is enforced principally by the Vienna Regional Court of Appeal, sitting as Cartel Court, and the Austrian Supreme Court, sitting as Cartel Court of Appeal.

1.1. ABUSE OF MARKET POWER

Austrian Postal Operator

The Austrian Cartel Court held that abusive conduct within the meaning of Section 35 of the Austrian Cartel Act requires a causal link between the dominant position and the abuse. A complainant (a private firm that distributes anonymous mass mailings, such as advertising and marketing materials) had argued that the Austrian postal operator abused its dominant position by distributing anonymous mass mailings through private mail boxes. Access to these mail boxes is restricted to the Austrian postal operator. The Cartel Court held that the postal operator's exclusive rights under Austrian law enabled the behavior in question and that there was therefore no causal link between the postal operator's dominant position and the alleged abusive conduct.

The Austrian Supreme Court overruled the Cartel Court's previous determination that abusive conduct within the meaning of Section 34 of the Austrian Cartel Act requires a causal link between the dominant position and the abuse. In conformity with the European Court of Justice's interpretation of Article 82 EC, the Supreme Court clarified that conduct is abusive if the methods employed by the dominant undertaking are different from those found in normal competition and have the effect of weakening the competition still existing in the market. There is no additional requirement of a causal link between the dominant position and the abusive conduct. Despite this holding, the Supreme Court nevertheless rejected arguments from the complainant that the Austrian postal operator abused its dominant position by distributing anonymous mass mailings through private mailboxes. The Austrian Postal Act gives the postal operator exclusive rights to access private mailboxes. By accessing private mailboxes to distribute mass mailings the Austrian postal operator did not, however, unjustifiably exercise power deriving from its dominant position on the market for reserved postal services in the related

Part II: National Competition Developments

market for the delivery of anonymous mass mailings, according to the Supreme Court. Rather, companies' and consumers' need for reliable delivery was held to justify the postal operator's distribution of anonymous mass mailings through private mailboxes.

Non-Cash Payment Systems

The Cartel Court issued an injunction against two major Austrian banks (the identities of which remain confidential), ordering them to allow the applicant, the operator of a direct-debiting point-of-sale payment system, to collect and process data stored on debit cards issued by the banks. In order to handle payments on its system, the applicant collects customers' bank account numbers and bank identification numbers at its point-of-sale terminals. Electronic collection of this data from customers' debit cards is indispensable for the system's operation.

The Cartel Court held that the two banks have a dominant position on the Austrian market for non-cash payment services. Under the Austrian Cartel Act, a company is dominant if, among other reasons, it enjoys a "very superior" market position *vis-à-vis* its customers or suppliers. The Cartel Court's finding rested on the fact that more than a quarter of the applicant's transactions are effected through debit cards issued by the two banks.

The Cartel Court concluded that the banks abused their dominant position by charging the applicant excessive interchange fees of ATS 3.80 per transaction, plus an annual lump sum interchange fee of ATS 3.9 million. The banks' actual costs did not exceed ATS 1.75 per transaction, and competitors' interchange fees were ATS 5.00 or less for each transaction. Under the injunction, the banks are to charge not more than an interchange fee of ATS 5.00 per transaction.

1.2. MERGERS AND ACQUISITIONS

Format/profil

The Austrian Cartel Court approved the acquisition of a controlling interest in KURIER Magazine Publishing GmbH by the News Group, the largest (in terms of share of readers) Austrian weekly news magazine publisher, subject to conditions.

The Austrian weekly news magazine market is highly concentrated, essentially consisting of three magazines: *News*, *Format*, and *profil*. *News* and *Format* are published by the News Group, and together account for 48% of readers; *profil*, which is owned by KURIER, accounts for 11% of readers. The concentration resulted in a near-monopoly in the Austrian weekly news magazine market.

The News Group relied on the "failing company defense," arguing that (i) *profil* would in the near future be forced to exit the market if not acquired by another entity, (ii) the News Group would take over the market share of *profil* if it exited the market, and (iii) no other potential purchaser of *profil* would result in fewer restraints on competition.

The Cartel Court rejected this defense on factual grounds. However, it found that several factors would reduce the risk of the News Group abusing its dominant position. First, readers are protected through the Consumer Protection and the Unfair Competition Acts. Second, weekly news magazines are not essential goods, and there is significant indirect competitive pressure.

Thus, the Cartel Court's main concern was not potential for abuse of a dominant position, but the prospect that the concentration could impair media diversity, which would oblige prohibition of a media concentration under Section 42c(5) of the Cartel Act. However, the Cartel Court found that ensuring the economic survival of *profil*, together with its editorial independence, would serve the interests of media diversity better than prohibiting the concentration. It therefore approved the concentration subject to three conditions:

1. The news magazine *profil* must continue to exist as a fully independent news magazine.

2. The production of *profil* must not be ceased prior to January 1, 2006.

3. Should the acquirer intend to cease the production of *profil* after December 12, 2005, it must notify the Cartel Court and provide evidence that serious sales efforts were futile and that *profil* is not economically viable.

Linde-Verlag/Wolters Kluwer

On December 17, the Austrian Supreme Court annulled a decision of the Cartel Court prohibiting, for the first time, a concentration in Austria, and referred the case back to the Cartel Court. The concentration concerned the proposed acquisition of Linde-Verlag by Wolters Kluwer. Wolters Kluwer currently holds 40% of the shares in Manz Verlag, a major Austrian publisher of legal publications with a market share of around 30%.

The Cartel Court had found on August 30 that the acquisition of Linde-Verlag, a publisher with a 20-25% share in the Austrian market for legal publications, would have strengthened Wolters Kluwer's dominant position in Austria. The parties argued that the market shares of Manz Verlag should not be attributed to Wolters Kluwer because Wolters Kluwer only held a minority stake in and had no decisive influence over Manz Verlag. (In an interesting procedural sidenote, the Cartel Court also rejected the parties' submission that the failure to notify the parties of a prohibition decision within the 5-month waiting period vitiated the decision, holding that the prohibition had been "issued", though not served on the parties, within the required time frame.)

The Supreme Court first considered whether the finding of a "concentration" for purposes of Section 41(1) no. 3 of the Austrian Cartel Act (concerning the acquisition or possession of a minority stake of at least 25%) required, in addition to the 25% shareholding, the exercise of decisive influence by the minority shareholder. It found that such decisive influence was not necessary, since a 25% shareholding already indicates a certain amount of economic influence. According to the Supreme Court, the concept of "concentration" should be read broadly in order to leave open the possibility of reviewing problematic cases.

The Supreme Court held, however, that the Cartel Court should have considered whether Wolters Kluwer had decisive influence over Manz Verlag in assessing whether the concentration would create or strengthen a dominant position. The Supreme Court therefore annulled the decision and required the Cartel Court to consider, on remand, whether Wolters Kluwer is indeed able to influence Manz Verlag's major decisions regarding investments, production, distribution and so forth. It noted that the actual exercise of such decisive influence is not required to attribute Manz Verlag's market share to Wolters Kluwer; the mere ability to do so would suffice. The Supreme Court stated further that, should the market share of Manz Verlag be attributable to Wolters Kluwer, the rebuttable presumption of dominance under Section 34(1) no. 1 of the Austrian Cartel Act (30% or higher market share) would apply.

Procedurally, the Supreme Court held that the referral would restart the regular 5-month period before the Cartel Court. While the Austrian Cartel Act is silent as to the duration of the review period upon referral, in making this determination the Supreme Court applied, by analogy, Article 10(5) of the EC Merger Regulation (pursuant to which the review periods under the EC Merger Regulation reset on the date on which the Court of Justice annuls a Commission decision).

1.3. JOINT VENTURES

Cooperative and Concentrative Joint Ventures

Under Section 41(2) of the Austrian Cartel Act, the creation of a joint venture qualifies as a concentration subject to merger control if the joint venture (i) performs on a lasting basis all the functions of an autonomous economic entity and

(ii) does not give rise to coordination of competitive behavior among the parent companies or between the parents and the joint venture.

The Austrian Cartel Court confirmed that Section 41(2) is to be interpreted in accordance with the principles established under the EC Merger Regulation prior to the abolition at the EU level of the distinction between cooperative and concentrative joint ventures. In particular, contrary to the plain wording of Section 41(2), coordination between parent companies and the joint venture is relevant only insofar as it is an instrument for producing or reinforcing coordination between the parent companies. Thus, the fact that one of the parents remains active in the joint venture's market does not preclude a joint venture from qualifying as a concentrative joint venture. Furthermore, the Cartel Court accepted a *de minimis* exception pursuant to which the parents will not be deemed active in the joint venture's market if they retain only minor activities in that market.

2. BELGIUM

This section reviews developments concerning the Competition Law of July 1, 1999, which is enforced principally by the Competition Service and the Competition Council.

2.1. ABUSE OF MARKET POWER

BVBA Incine/NV Rendac

On February 2, BVBA Incine filed a complaint with the Council and requested interim measures against NV Rendac. Incine and Rendac provide services in Belgium for the collection and processing of animal carcasses. Rendac also provides services for the collection and processing of farm animal carcasses, a market in which it has a 100% market share.

In 1998, the Belgian government decided to compensate companies providing farm animal processing services for losses incurred by the government's stringent measures intended to contain the Belgian dioxin crisis and mad cow disease. Incine's complaint asserts that Rendac used this compensation to cross-subsidize its non-farm animal processing business, in which Rendac has a market share of approximately 35% and competes against Incine.

The Council determined that Rendac holds a *prima facie* dominant position on the market for non-farm animal processing services. The Council relied on four main factors in making this assessment: (i) Rendac's 35% share of this market; (ii) Rendac's 100% share in the related market for farm animal processing services; (iii) Rendac has few competitors in the market for non-farm animal processing services; and (iv) Rendac has financial and technological resources at its disposal that are superior to those generally available to market players. The Council then concluded that Rendac abused its dominant position on the market for non-farm animal processing services by cross-subsidizing its activities on that market with the government's compensation for its services in the farm animal processing services market.

The Council's finding that Rendac is dominant in the non-farm animal processing services market – where it has just a 35% share – is surprising. Finding abuse in a cross-subsidization case ordinarily only requires evidence of a dominant position on the *subsidizing* market (*i.e.*, farm animal processing services, the market from which the additional revenue is derived); the firm's position on the subsidized market is ordinarily immaterial. By focusing on Rendac's position on the subsidized market, the Council – without explanation – changes the traditional standard of scrutiny on abuses of dominant position through cross-subsidization. The decision thus creates uncertainty regarding the Council's future application of the standard.

2.2. MERGERS AND ACQUISITIONS

Vinci/Groupe GTM

In the *Vinci* and *Groupe GTM* case, the Council declined to impose a fine on the parties for failing to notify a concentration within the mandatory one-month deadline. The Council held that in this case the late filing was justified for the following reasons: (i) the parties had first had negotiations with the European Commission with respect to the potential application of EC rules; (ii) the parties had difficulties in gathering all the necessary information during the summer holiday season; and (iii) the notifying parties had informed the Service about the transaction before the one-month period had expired.

De Beers/Rio Tinto/Ashton Mining; P&O/Antwerp Combined Terminals

In two rulings, the Competition Council held that turnover should be allocated for jurisdictional purposes to the location where transactions are entered into. This position is at odds with the approach followed by many competition authorities, including the European Commission, which allocates turnover based on the location of the customer at the time of the transaction.

The first case involved three diamond producers, De Beers, Ashton Mining and Rio Tinto, none of which sold large volumes of goods to end-customers in Belgium. Their only nexus to Belgium was the Antwerp Diamond Exchange, the world's largest diamond market, where all three firms did significant amounts of business.

In assessing its jurisdiction in the context of merger proposals involving these firms, the Council ruled that sales performed on the Antwerp Diamond Exchange should be allocated to Belgium for purposes of jurisdictional calculation. First, sale contracts on the exchange are entered into in Antwerp, which is also the place of delivery of the goods. Second, all competition for such sales takes place on the exchange in Antwerp, where supply and demand meet. Third, most customers, even if located in another country, are represented by a broker in Antwerp. Accordingly, the Competition Council held that the location of the end-customer is irrelevant to competition and thus to the geographic allocation of turnover. The critical factor is the location where the transaction takes place.

In the second case, *P&O/Antwerp Combined Terminals*, the Council held that turnover associated with harbor services rendered in Antwerp is Belgian turnover for jurisdictional purposes. The parties had argued that, since most of their clients were not based in Belgium, this turnover should not be attributed to Belgium. However, the Council rejected this reasoning for reasons similar to those cited in *De Beers/Ashton Mining/Rio Tinto*. The Council's opinion also contains the following *obiter dictum*: "The relevant turnover is the one reflected in a company's financial statements. It would be impossible for the Council to verify the accuracy of geographic allocation if the parties did not report the figure stated in their financial statements."

The Council's position has been heavily criticized for creating uncertainty as to the Council's future approach toward geographic allocation of turnover.

2.3. POLICY AND PROCEDURE

"New Hearing" Rule in Merger Proceedings

In 2000, De Beers and Rio Tinto were competing for corporate control of Ashton Mining through takeover bids. Both De Beers and Rio Tinto notified their proposed acquisitions of Ashton to the Belgian authorities. On October 18, 2000, the Competition Council cleared Rio Tinto's bid and opened a second-phase investigation into the De Beers bid.

Following this decision, De Beers formally requested a new hearing, basing its claim on Article 772 of the Belgian Judicial Code. Article 772 provides that, after a formal ruling has been issued, parties have the right to request a new hearing upon discovery of a "new and essential" element.

In response, the Competition Council held that general rules of civil procedure apply to all procedures before the Competition Council, including merger control proceedings. However, the Council rejected De Beers's request for a new hearing on grounds that no "new and essential" element had been raised. At the same time, the Council expressed doubt as to whether a decision to open a second-phase investigation is a formal ruling to which the Article 772 "new hearing" rule can in principle apply. Rio Tinto subsequently acquired Ashton Mining.

Removal of Members of the Competition Service

In a request for interim measures by the Unie der Belgische Ambulancediensten against the Belgian Red Cross, the Unie applied to have two members of the Competition Service removed from that case because of alleged prejudiced decision-making. The Council determined that the law does not grant it the power to remove Competition Service members under such circumstances.

Council Annual Report

On September 12, 2001, the General Assembly of the Competition Council approved the Council's annual report for 2000. The annual report focuses on the repercussions of the new Belgian Competition law of July 1, 1999, on the Council's year-2000 practice.

Intervention of the Competition Council before the Court of Appeals

Under the Competition Law, the Council has a right of intervention in appeals of Competition Council decisions brought by companies before the Court of Appeals. In the annual report, the Council notes that this procedural right could be criticized as an attempt to influence the Court's judgment. In light of this concern, the report declares that the Council will normally not make use of its right of intervention.

New Merger Notification Thresholds

Under the pre-1999 Competition Law, notification of concentrations was required if the parties' combined turnover in Belgium exceeded BEF 3 billion (approximately € 97 million) and the concentration would result in a market share above 25%. The new Competition Law requires notification whenever the aggregate turnover in Belgium of the parties exceeds € 40 million and the individual turnover in Belgium of at least two of the parties exceeds € 15 million.

In the annual report, the Council strongly criticized the abandonment under the new Competition Law of the market share-based threshold. Under the new system, a concentration between a company with a strong market position and considerable turnover and a company with Belgian turnover below € 15 million need not be reported. The report notes that, in many cases, such transactions might threaten effective competition. Similarly, transactions creating high market shares in relatively small markets may often go unreported under the new rule.

Part II: National Competition Developments

Non-reportable transactions are not, however, exempt from antitrust laws. To reduce the risk of competitive harm from non-reportable transactions, the Council is contemplating strengthening its capacity to examine non-reportable transactions.

3. DENMARK

This section reviews developments concerning the Danish Competition Act of June 10, 1997, enforced by the Competition Council assisted by the Competition Authority and the Competition Tribunal.

3.1. VERTICAL RESTRAINTS

Tryg Baltica

The Authority required Tryg Baltica (an insurance firm) and an advertising agency to abandon a contractual provision obliging the advertising agency not to carry out any tasks for any other insurance companies. Tryg Baltica is one of the largest Danish insurance companies, with a market share of 20% to 25%.

Den Almindelige Danske Lægeforening

On May 9, the Authority found that agreements between Den Almindelige Danske Lægeforening (the Organization of Danish Medicines, or ODM) and three pharmaceutical companies did not fall within the scope of Section 6 of the Act (prohibiting anti-competitive agreements). The agreements obliged ODM to sell advertising space to the three pharmaceutical companies on ODM's closed circuit network, Daddlenet, which is only accessible to ODM members (*i.e.*, doctors). The contracts prohibit ODM from offering third parties similar advertising space on the network during the one-year contract term. The Authority approved the agreements, finding that (i) other pharmaceutical companies have adequate means besides Daddlenet to market their products in Denmark; (ii) the one-year term of the contracts was relatively short and did not exclude ODM from entering into new contracts during the contract period that would take effect immediately after the contract period; (iii) the agreements were of relatively minor economic importance; and (iv) the contracts were entered into following an open auction process.

Part II: National Competition Developments

Carlsberg

On October 31, the Council adopted a decision requiring Carlsberg to amend its distributor agreements on the Danish market.

Carlsberg holds an 80% share of the Danish market for labeled beers and a 70% share of the total beer market in Denmark. Carlsberg distributes its own products throughout most of the country, with the exception of some isolated areas. In these isolated areas, Carlsberg appointed exclusive distributors, requiring them to undertake not to distribute competing products. The Council found that these exclusivity provisions raised unacceptable barriers to entry for new competitors. Carlsberg was required to remove the agreements' exclusivity provisions.

Danish Football Association

Also on October 31, the Council decided that the Danish Football Association should amend its exclusive agreement with the two Danish public television stations, DR and TV 2. According to the agreement, DR and TV 2 were together granted an exclusive right for a period of 8 years to broadcast the Danish national team's home-field matches. It was left for the two stations to divide the transmissions between them. While recognizing that special rules apply to transmission of football matches (see, *e.g.*, the EC Directive on Television Without Frontiers); the Council found that an exclusive agreement lasting for 8 years was unacceptable in light of the EC Commission's practice under EU competition rules. The Council stated that a two-year exclusive term would be acceptable. This would cover the present agreement's remaining term.

Real Estate Franchise Chain

In a further decision on October 31, the Council authorized a set of standard franchise agreements used by the chain of real estate agents called "home", which holds a 20% share of the Danish real estate market. The agreements in question required home franchisees not to undertake competing activities in the exclusive area granted to the franchisee, plus a zone of 10 km surrounding that area, for one year after termination of the agreement. The Council found that, given home's market share, the agreements in question fell within the Danish executive order concerning group exemption of vertical agreements (which is identical to the EC Commission block exemption on vertical agreements). In connection with the Council's clearance of the agreements, however, home agreed to limit the geographical scope of the no-compete clause to the exclusive area granted to the franchisee.

3.2. ABUSE OF MARKET POWER

Dansk Kørelærer Union

Dansk Kørelærer Union (the Organization of Danish Driving Instructors, or DKU) includes 80% to 90% of Danish driving instructors as members and publishes the only magazine for this group in Denmark. DKU also produces various material used in connection with the education of driving pupils. A third party, Trafiktesten.dk produced a CD-ROM that could be used as an alternative to the material produced by DKU. DKU refused to accept advertisements from Trafiktesten in the magazine distributed to its members, and Trafiktesten complained that such refusal constituted an abuse of DKU's dominant position. The Authority disagreed. In accordance with the Tribunal's decision of September 29, 1998 (*Dansk Sportsdykker Forbund vs. Konkurrencerådet*), abuse of a dominant position exists only if "special conditions" are present. The fact that DKU's magazine was the only one of its kind in Denmark did not, in the opinion of the Authority, amount to a "special condition."

Opel Danmark

On November 28, the Competition Council declared that Opel Danmark's bonus scheme in relation to the sale of spare parts did not constitute an abuse of a dominant position. The decision followed the Competition Authority's May 30 report on the automotive sector, which concluded that auto manufacturers' use of fidelity rebates was an important factor in the protection of the market for spare parts produced by the original equipment manufacturers. However, the report had found that Opel Danmark's bonus scheme constituted an abuse of a dominant position, as the scheme was linked to individual purchase targets set according to purchasing levels in the previous year, and the size of the bonus was calculated on a progressive scale. After negotiating with the Competition Authority, Opel Danmark undertook to change the bonus scheme for 2002 so that the bonuses would be paid quarterly to each dealer according to a sliding scale based on the actual purchases made. The Competition Council found that this amended bonus scheme was in accordance with the Competition Act.

Ruko

On December 19, the Competition Council declared that Ruko A/S, the dominant supplier on the Danish market for locks (with an 80% share), had abused its dominant position. Ruko's dominance was reinforced by the existence of several barriers to foreign companies' entry into the Danish lock market, including in particular the fact that builders and architects generally use a special Scandinavian standard that effectively excludes non-Scandinavian products from the market.

The Council identified two principal abusive practices. First, Ruko's discount system treated distributors unequally. In particular, one distributor (which had also marketed products competing with Ruko's) obtained a smaller discount on locks than other distributors because it did not also purchase certain other items (such as furnishings and door handles) from Ruko. Further, by giving varying discounts to distributors in relation to large building projects, Ruko was found to have discriminated among its distributors and consequently placed them in unequal competitive positions. Second, Ruko was found to have prevented the resale of locks that it had sold at special prices to bulk purchasers, with the intention of compartmentalizing the market. The Competition Council ordered Ruko to alter its discount system and to desist from measures restricting the resale of its products.

3.3. MERGERS AND ACQUISITIONS

DONG/Naturgas Sjælland

On February 28, the Council approved the merger of DONG (a government-owned North Sea oil and gas producer) and Naturgas Sjælland (a regional Danish gas company), subject to three conditions:

1. DONG must modify certain of its gas supply contracts with electricity plants to allow the plants to contract with other suppliers beginning no later than December 31, 2009.

2. DONG must offer open access to its gas transportation network according to published standard prices, terms, and conditions. This is intended to increase market transparency and benefit customers, and will permit foreign gas suppliers to make use of DONG's network and compete in Denmark.

3. DONG must offer customers and competitors access to its two gas storage facilities in Denmark.

In connection with its approval, the Council recommended that the Minister of Environment and Energy open the Danish gas market to foreign suppliers sooner, and to a wider extent, than is currently anticipated provided for under applicable legislation. The legislation permitted foreign suppliers to provide up to 30% of Danish gas consumption in 2000, and would increase this threshold to 38% by August 2003 and to 43% by August 2008. However, approximately 15-20% of Danish gas consumption is covered by long-term supply agreements between DONG and electricity plants, and foreign suppliers' penetration of the Danish market is expected to take longer than contemplated.

AB/Provinzial

On May 30, the Competition Council approved the purchase by the insurance company Alm. Brand af 1792 G/S (AB) of Provinzial Brandkasse (Provinzial), a division of a competing insurance company. The parties' combined share of the market for general insurance in Denmark was 11%, and the Council found accordingly that the transaction would not create a dominant position. Within certain insurance segments, the combined market share was higher (up to 35%) but the Council found that there was no substantial overlap in the segments where the parties' combined shares were highest, and thus cleared the transaction without conditions.

As part of the notification, the parties requested clearance for a non-compete clause that prohibited the seller from competing with the transferred activities for three years. The parties had argued that AB would take over Provinzial's special know-how relating to a computer system that had been developed for Provinzial's employees and distribution channels. AB had not previously used third-party agents to distribute its products, and argued that the computer system involved unique know-how that justified a three-year non-compete restriction.

The Council rejected this argument, finding that a three-year non-compete period could not be justified as ancillary to the transaction and stating that only a two-year non-compete could be found ancillary. However, the Council found that as a result of the parties' modest combined market shares, the restriction would not have any appreciable effect on the market, and accordingly deemed the non-compete clause to fall outside the scope of Section 6 of the Act (prohibiting anti-competitive agreements).

Part II: National Competition Developments

Højgaard & Schultz/Monberg & Thorsen

The Council also cleared the establishment of HMT Entreprenør A/S, created by a merger between two major Danish contracting firms, Højgaard & Schultz A/S and Monberg & Thorsen A/S. The Council examined the transaction's effects on a number of markets in Denmark but found that it would not create any dominant positions. Notably, despite adopting a national market definition, the Council took particular note of competition that Danish enterprises face from Swedish contracting firms.

Carlsberg/Coca-Cola Bottlers

The Chairman of the Council and the chief officer of the Authority together approved Carlsberg's acquisition of the Coca-Cola bottlers in Denmark, finding that the transaction would not create any dominant position on the Danish market. The decision was rendered pursuant to Section 7(4) of the Rules of Procedure of the Council, whereby the Chairman of the Council and the chief officer of the Authority may together render decisions that cannot await the next Council meeting.

3.4. POLICY AND PROCEDURE

Agreement between Nordic Competition Authorities

The competition authorities in Denmark, Iceland and Norway signed an agreement on March 16 with a view to increase cooperation. The agreement provides for exchange of information, including confidential information, between the authorities in cases of mutual interest. This includes merger cases, where the agencies consider it necessary to strengthen cooperation because of the close links between their respective national markets. In addition, the authorities anticipate that closer cooperation will facilitate their ability to fight cross-border cartels.

Nordic Competition Meeting

The Competition Authorities of Denmark, Finland, the Faeroe Islands, Greenland, Iceland, Norway and Sweden met on September 6-7 to discuss matters of common interest. At the meeting, the authorities decided to undertake a common investigation of the aviation sector, in which all of the authorities perceive competition problems. The authorities consider that a coordinated position will facilitate identification and resolution of these problems.

Proposed Amendments to Competition Act

The Danish Government has proposed the following amendments to the Danish Competition Act: [113]

- Increases in fines for breach of the Competition Act. According to the Competition Act, fines for breaching the act are set in accordance with general Danish legal principles for imposing fines for breaches of commercial regulations. Fines are currently set by reference to the seriousness and duration of the breach with, in practice, a maximum limit of DKK 3 million (€ 400,000). Under the proposed amendment, fines would be raised to a level equal to those imposable under EC competition law.

- Increased powers for the Competition Council to comment on competition restrictions resulting from public regulation. At present, the Competition Council cannot interfere with restrictive trade practices that are a direct or necessary consequence of regulation. The proposal would retain this limitation but would entitle the Competition Council to request from the relevant minister a ruling on whether a restrictive trade practice is a direct or necessary consequence of public regulation. It is envisaged that the minister would be obliged to respond to such requests within four weeks, subject to possible extension of this time limit by the Competition Council.

- Authority for the Competition Council to comment on regulations that it finds inappropriate and to advise the Government on how to promote a competitive environment within Denmark. In response to such comments and advice, the relevant minister would be obliged to negotiate with the Competition Council and to respond to the Competition Council's statement within four months.

- Increased investigative powers. Technical provisions regulating investigations may be amended to give the Competition Authority access to additional data sources, such as externally sited computers, during its investigations. Additional powers in relation to the removal of documents, computers, and other media for copying are also being proposed.

- Clarification of joint venture rules. The proposal recommends clarifying the application of Article 6 of the Competition Act (equivalent to Article 81

---

[113] These amendments were ultimately adopted on May 29, 2002 and will enter into force on August 1, 2002.

EC) to joint ventures. As a result of the absence of Danish merger control rules at the time, under the 1997 predecessor to the current Competition Act it was unclear whether the Act's prohibition on anti-competitive agreements applied to cooperative joint ventures in the same way as does Article 81 EC (according to which anti-competitive joint ventures not falling within the EC Merger Regulation can be scrutinized). Some ambiguity on this issue still exists under the current Act, even though the intention is that Article 6 should be applied consistently with Article 81 EC. Accordingly, the proposal would make clear that cooperative joint ventures not falling under the EC Merger Regulation may be caught by Article 6 with the same implications as if they were caught by Article 81 EC.

4. FRANCE

This section reviews developments concerning Part IV of the French Commercial Code on Free Prices and Competition, which is enforced by the Competition Council and the Ministry of Financial and Economic Affairs.

4.1. VERTICAL RESTRAINTS

Canal+

In a May 11 decision that ended five months of interim measure proceedings, the Competition Council ordered Canal+ to delete exclusivity clauses from its standard contract used for the purchase of pay-per-view (PPV) broadcasting rights to "new" French feature films. This order applies until the Competition Council reaches a final decision on the merits of the case.

This decision is the latest episode in the legal battle started in 1997 by TPS (a direct-to-home operator controlled by France Telecom, Suez, TF1 and M6) and Multivision (a TPS subsidiary operating a PPV service distributed by TPS) against Canal+, the leading French pay-TV group (which operates the Canal+ channel as well as CanalSatellite, a direct-to-home operator, and the NC Numéricâble cable network).

In December 1998, the Competition Council found that Canal+ had illegally conditioned its purchase of French film broadcasting rights for pay-TV on French film producers not selling to PPV services the right to broadcast those films before or during their broadcast by Canal+. The Competition Council held that such practices were an abuse of a dominant position. The Competition Council's decision and order to cease the abusive activity were later upheld by the Paris Court of Appeal.

According to TPS and Multivision, Canal+ did not comply with the order. In January 2001, they filed a new complaint with the Competition Council, alleging that Canal+ continued to prevent third parties from acquiring French film PPV broadcasting rights by purchasing most of these rights through Kiosque (a wholly-owned subsidiary of Canal+ providing PPV services) on an exclusive basis for a 24-month period. According to the complainants, because of the historical relationships between Canal+ and the French cinema industry, French producers are inclined to sell PPV broadcasting rights to Canal+/Kiosque rather than to TPS/Multivision. The complainants also alleged that the 24-month exclusivity period was excessive because Kiosque broadcasts films only for three-month periods before removing them from its broadcast rotation.

Multivision and TPS also challenged in the new complaint an agreement concluded in May 2000 between Canal+ and several organizations representing the French cinema industry. This agreement gives Canal+ an extended "window" of 18 months for the exclusive broadcasting of the most expensive (and, it is assumed, the most desirable) feature films instead of the 12-month period granted for other films.

The complaint alleged that such an agreement made it virtually impossible for third-party PPV operators to have access to these films even after their broadcast on Canal+, since at the end of the 18-month "window," free-access channels may begin broadcasting such films.

Under French law, interim measures may be imposed if (i) the complaint seems *prima facie* well-founded, and (ii) there is a serious and immediate threat to the overall economy, the market concerned, the complainant's interest or consumer welfare.

The Competition Council found that it was *prima facie* possible that the combination of these two agreements constituted abuse of a dominant position by Canal+.

Regarding the "serious and immediate threat" condition required for interim measures to be ordered, the Competition Council found that the alleged financial difficulties of Multivision were real. The Council also observed that due to the difficulties faced by Multivision in purchasing PPV rights for "new" French feature films, it could not comply with national regulations requiring that French feature films constitute at least 40% of the movies shown on a channel. This could lead to the elimination of one of the two French PPV operators, which would undoubtedly harm competition in the sector and substantially reduce consumer choice. Finally, the Council held that Multivision's exit from the market could endanger TPS's direct-to-home options.

The Competition Council therefore ordered Canal+ and Kiosque to refrain from acquiring, directly or indirectly, exclusive PPV broadcasting rights on "new" French feature films until the Competition Council renders its decision on the merits.

Benetton

On September 24, the Competition Council dismissed complaints by former retailers of Benetton clothing against the manufacturer.[114] The retailers had made two principal allegations: first, that Benetton had required the retailers to engage specific firms to design their shops; and second, that Benetton had fixed the resale prices of its products.

Regarding the first claim, the Competition Council found that there was insufficient evidence to support the allegations. The Council noted further that, in any case, the relevant market (which was found to be even wider than the market for shop designing in general) was too large to be significantly affected by this practice.

In support of their second claim, some retailers complained that Benetton had pre-marked retail prices on its products, which prevented the retailers from changing the price. The Competition Council noted that Article L 420-1 of the Commercial Code prohibits manufacturers from setting fixed or minimum resale prices for its products (although it allows setting maximum or recommended prices). In assessing Benetton's actions, the council first found that (particularly given the conflicting testimony from various retailers) there was insufficient evidence to establish that Benetton effectively imposed the resale prices of its products on its distributors. The pre-marked prices appeared to function only as recommendations. Second, the Council found that, even if Benetton had imposed fixed or minimum resale prices, this would not have significantly affected competition on the relevant market (retail clothing sales in France). Since Benetton's share of this market was only 2.38%, the Council found that even vertical price restraints would not have had a "substantial effect" on competition.

This is the first time the Council has used the concept of substantial effect in the context of vertical price restraints. French competition law does not expressly require a showing of "substantial effect" in vertical restraints cases. However, it appears that the Council has now rejected the idea of *per se* violations in vertical price restraint cases. The decision suggests that market share is the main criterion that the Competition Council employs in seeking to identify whether vertical restraints have a "substantial effect" on competition.

---

[114] On April 2, 2002, the Court of Appeal of Paris rejected the appeal introduced by the Minister of the Economy on October 23, 2001 against the Competition Council decision of September 24, 2001.

Based on these findings, the Council considered that there was no need to continue the proceedings and dismissed the complaint.

4.2. HORIZONTAL AGREEMENTS

Banking Sector Cartel

The antitrust division of the Ministry of Economy recently published an important Competition Council case decided on September 19, 2000. The Council imposed the highest fines since its creation in 1987 on six French retail banks: FF 450 million (€ 68.6 million) on Crédit Agricole, FF 250 million (€ 38 million) on BNP, FF 250 million (€ 38 million) on Société Générale, FF 100 million (€ 15 million) on Crédit Lyonnais, FF 70 million (€ 10.6 million) on Caisses d'Epargne, and FF 10 million (€ 1.5 million) on Crédit Mutuel.

The Competition Council found that the six banks participated in a cartel in the real estate loan sector during 1993 and 1994. The cartel consisted of a "non-aggression pact" whereby a participating bank would refuse to offer better conditions to another cartel member's customer who was seeking to renegotiate his or her loan terms.

In the years 1993 and 1994, outstanding French real estate loans represented FF 600 billion (€ 91.5 billion). During this period, only FF 40 billion (€ 6.09 billion) (about seven percent of the total) were actually renegotiated by the banks; the Council thought this rate abnormally low. This, together with various statements made by bank executives and documents discovered during investigations, convinced the Competition Council that the banks had behaved collusively.

The Council's finding contradicted the recommendations of the AFB (the French banking trade association) and the *Commission Bancaire* (the French banking regulatory body), both of which observed that banking is highly competitive with low margins. The Council also rejected the defendants' argument that "tacit collusion" between the banks explained their reluctance to bid aggressively for each other's borrowers. The banks maintained that this was not the result of explicit collusion but rather the fear of retaliation. However, given that the banks held numerous meetings on these issues, the Council rejected this defense.

This decision is one of very few in the Council's case law concerning the banking sector and shows that the Council is willing to exercise its jurisdiction in all economic sectors, even those supervised by other regulatory authorities.

Accor/Sodhexo/Chèque-Déjeuner

The Competition Council found that the three main issuers of restaurant vouchers – Accor, Sodhexo Chèques et Cartes de Service, and Chèque-Déjeuner – had established a market-sharing and price-fixing cartel. Under the restaurant voucher system, the issuing companies sell vouchers to employers who, in turn, sell them to their employees below nominal value. Employees may pay for meals with the vouchers, and the restaurants accepting the vouchers are later reimbursed by the issuing companies at the vouchers' nominal value. The restaurants also pay a commission to the issuing company.

The Council found that the three issuing companies had agreed to allocate the market and not to increase their respective market shares. Among the sanctioned practices, the issuing companies agreed not to tender for the same bids for public employers, and not to solicit each others' private sector clients without prior approval and to allocate private sector commissions. Finally, the companies also agreed to apply the same commission to restaurants accepting vouchers in order to prevent any competition among themselves.

The Competition Council imposed fines of FF 4 million (€ 609,796) on Accor, FF 2.5 million (€ 381,122) on Chèque-Déjeuner, and FF 2 million (€ 304,898) on Sodhexo.

Concrete Industry Cartel

The Competition Council fined fifteen companies in the prefabricated concrete sector a total of FF 9.7 million (approximately € 1.5 million). The Council found that the companies had operated as a cartel, engaging in market sharing, establishing quotas, and setting artificially high prices for prefabricated concrete. In support of its decision, the Council cited the companies' parallel behavior and a large body of evidence indicating actual coordination of activity.

The Council based the amount of the fine on the number of companies involved, the seriousness of the violations, the increase in prices of material used, the non-elasticity of demand for the relevant products, and the damage to the economy caused by the coordinated behavior.

Construction Industry Cartel

The Competition Council fined eight construction companies a total of FF 10.4 million (approximately € 1.58 million). The Council held that seven of these companies had impermissibly exchanged information, resulting in market allocation

Part II: National Competition Developments

for road renewal projects in the Gard area of France. Moreover, the Council found that the same companies had agreed to a concerted bid for work on a school construction project in Nîmes.

4.3. ABUSE OF MARKET POWER

France Télécom

Following its investigation of a case referred by the Authority for Telecommunications Regulation, the Competition Council found that France Télécom (FT) abused its dominant position in several telecommunications markets in 1999 by hindering access by other providers to the market for telecom services for business customers. First, FT offered rebates to business customers based on their total communications volume (including local and national services). By linking its tariffs to the customer's total calling volume, FT impermissibly gave customers incentives to select FT's offer for regional and inter-city calls (a market in which FT faces competition) in order to receive greater rebates on local calls (a market on which FT had a monopoly). Second, the Council found that FT abused its dominant position in the market for calls from fixed phones to mobile phones. FT could offer very low tariffs in this market because it did not have to pay a connection fee to access the Itineris mobile phone network. FT's low tariff functioned as a barrier against entry to the market. The Competition Council imposed a fine of FF 40 million (€ 6.1 million) for these practices. This is the first litigation referral from the Authority for Telecommunications Regulation and is the first time that FT has been fined for abusive practices following liberalization of the French telecommunications market.

4.4. MERGERS AND ACQUISITIONS

Boeing/Jeppesen Group

On July 4, the Minister of Financial and Economic Affairs approved the acquisition by Boeing of the Jeppesen Group, subject to certain conditions. Jeppesen is an American company that provides flight information services such as cartography and aerial navigation services. As part of the approval, the Minister imposed a five-year injunction on both companies, pursuant to which Jeppessen must refrain from disclosing any non-public information concerning Airbus or any of its clients, and Boeing must refrain from trying to obtain such information from Jeppessen.

Jeppesen's navigation services are used by almost every airline in the world, on both Airbus and Boeing aircraft. Providing such services requires Jeppesen to have an exhaustive knowledge of the aircraft, including confidential information. The Minister found that confidentiality agreements signed by the parties would be insufficient to protect against the disclosure to Boeing of sensitive information about Airbus aircraft. Accordingly, Boeing and Jeppesen must present to the Minister a plan providing for reduced information transfer from airlines to Jeppesen.

4.5. POLICY AND PROCEDURE

Amendments to Competition Law

After more than a year of parliamentary debate, the Law on New Economic Regulations, which substantially modifies French competition rules by introducing, among other things, a mandatory pre-merger notification system and leniency measures for whistle-blowers, was enacted on May 15. Most of the law's provisions were immediately applicable, but the new notification system applied only to transactions entered into after the publication of an implementing decree.[115]

---

[115] On April 30, 2002 an Implementing Decree of the Law on New Economic Regulations was adopted. The decree set May 18, 2002 as the date on which the new merger control rules, including a mandatory pre-merger notification regime, enter into force.

5. GERMANY

This section reviews developments concerning the Act against Restraints of Competition of 1957 (the Competition Act), which is enforced by the Federal Cartel Office (the FCO), the cartel offices of the individual German Länder, and the Ministry of Economic Affairs.

5.1. HORIZONTAL AGREEMENTS

Ready-Mixed Concrete Industry Cartel

Between August 2000 and February 2001, the FCO imposed a record fine of approximately DM 370 million (€ 194 million) on ready-mixed concrete firms involved in illegal quota agreements over several years in Eastern Germany. All of the leading companies in the sector were involved. By the end of the year, fines amounting to DM 280 million (€ 143 million), became final. The FCO is currently undertaking further investigations into suspected quota and price-fixing agreements in the ready-mixed concrete sector in other regions in Germany.

Inter-bank Charge for Eurocheque Card Payments

The German Central Credit Committee (*Zentraler Kreditausschuss*) withdrew notification of its intention to introduce an inter-bank charge for Eurocheque card payments. The FCO had informed the Credit Committee on March 7 that it was planning to oppose the introduction of the inter-bank charge. In taking this position, the FCO rejected the Credit Committee's argument that the banks were incurring losses with the Eurocheque direct payment system. FCO President Böge stated that, if this was true, the banks had to try to absorb or pass on the costs of competing against each other instead of jointly passing on the cost to the consumer through opaque charges.

5.2. ABUSE OF MARKET POWER

Electricity Sector Proceedings

On October 30, the FCO announced that it had opened proceedings against four electricity grid operators for charging excessive and arbitrary fees for the provision of "balancing energy" (energy required to match the amount of electricity fed into a network to the amount of electricity actually used at a certain point in time). The energy companies that control the large electricity grids hold a monopoly position with respect to the provision of balancing energy, since only they are able to disconnect and connect power plants at short notice. The FCO held that the four companies' pricing systems did not bear an apparent correlation between costs incurred and prices charged, and differed from the other two electricity grid companies' (RWE and E.ON) pricing systems, which were in line with competition law. The FCO did not accept the companies' defense that their pricing systems corresponded to the provisions of the "Electricity Association Agreement," a private agreement between the industry associations that are active in the energy sector that is aimed at regulating, in particular, network access. The FCO noted, however, that adherence to a private agreement could not justify a violation of antitrust law; the fact that the pricing systems were in line with the Electricity Association Agreement showed merely that the agreement did not conform with competition law. (See also below under 5.5. Policy and Procedure.)

5.3. MERGERS AND ACQUISITIONS

Goodyear/Michelin

On January 26, the FCO cleared implementation of RubberNetwork.com, the e-commerce platform proposed by rubber manufacturers Goodyear and Michelin. While the case did not pose any unique merger control issues, the FCO cleared the project only in the second phase after intense investigations regarding the proposed aggregation of demand with respect to non-strategic goods and services. In this respect, the FCO will continue to keep a close eye on how the platform develops in the future.

Kirch Group/EM.TV

On March 29, the FCO allowed the Kirch group to proceed with its planned acquisition of 49% of the outstanding shares in SPEED Investment Ltd. from EM.TV.

Together with Bernie Ecclestone's Bambino Trust, SPEED controls SLEC Holdings Ltd., which owns the world-wide marketing rights to Formula 1 auto racing. In the same context, the FCO also cleared the Kirch-financed exercise of a US$ 1 billion (€ 1.18 billion) option held by EM.TV/SPEED to buy an additional 25% of SLEC, thereby raising the SPEED stake in SLEC to 75%, with the remaining 25% being held by Bambino Trust. According to the FCO, the concentration will not give the Kirch group control over Formula 1 broadcasting rights in Germany, since the parties undertook to carve out these rights for specific licensing periods into separate companies and to sell these companies by auction in neutral and open procedures. As a result of this structure, any future acquisition of German Formula 1 broadcasting rights will be subject to merger control.

Callahan Associates/NetCologne

On April 11, the Düsseldorf Court of Appeals (*Oberlandesgericht*), the court competent for appeals against FCO decisions, enjoined the implementation of the proposed acquisition of Cologne telephone company NetCologne by Callahan Associates, which had been cleared by the FCO in February. NetCologne was to be integrated into Callahan affiliate Kabel NRW, which is jointly controlled by Callahan (55%) and Deutsche Telekom (45%). Upon motion of NetCologne competitor Primacom AG, the court expressed serious doubts regarding the soundness of the FCO's reasoning, which was based primarily on the arguments that, despite its 45% stake in Kabel NRW, Deutsche Telekom would not be able to influence business decisions in Kabel NRW, and that the acquisition of NetCologne would enable Callahan to develop Kabel NRW into a strong competitor of Deutsche Telekom in the telephone and internet lines market.

Lekkerland/Tobaccoland

On May 9, the Berlin Court of Appeals (*Kammergericht*) rendered the second of two landmark decisions finding that third parties are able to challenge directly FCO merger approval decisions. This decision concerned the merger of German food company Lekkerland and German tobacco products company Tobaccoland, which was approved by the FCO more than two years ago and has since been consummated. The Berlin Court of Appeals lifted the clearance decision and remanded it to the FCO, but, at the same time, permitted an appeal to the Federal Civil Court (*Bundesgerichtshof*).

It has been possible for third parties to bring lawsuits against second-phase merger clearance decisions since the sixth amendment to the Competition Act came into force on January 1, 1999. The April 11 decision of the Düsseldorf Court of Appeals in *Callahan/NetCologne* (see above) and the Berlin Court of Appeals decision are the first to apply this principle.

VEBA/VIAG; RWE/VEW

Both the European Commission and the FCO had cleared mergers between VEBA and VIAG and RWE and VEW in June/July 2000 conditioned upon divestiture of the participants' stakes in other German energy suppliers. In particular E.ON, the newly-named company resulting from the VEBA/VIAG merger, was ordered to sell its 49% stake in Berlin energy supplier BEWAG, and both E.ON and RWE undertook to sell their stakes in Eastern German energy supplier VEAG, in VEAG's lignite supplier Laubag, and in integrated Eastern German power supplier Envia.

These undertakings (which were imposed in parallel by the European Commission and the FCO) were aimed at creating, apart from the two merged entities, a third strong interconnected electric company that would – along with other competitors such as Energie Baden-Württemberg, strong municipal utilities, and domestic and foreign newcomers – exert strong competitive pressure on the two market leaders, E.ON. and the new merged RWE.

First, E.ON agreed to sell its 49% stake in BEWAG to Hamburg energy supplier HEW. Although this sale was challenged by BEWAG's minority stakeholder Mirant (formerly Southern Energy), which alleged that the sale violated a right of first refusal, the matter was settled following a nine-month arbitration proceeding with an agreement providing that HEW acquire E.ON's 49% shareholding in BEWAG, then resell 17% to Mirant, so that HEW and Mirant will each hold 43% in BEWAG. In the FCO's view, BEWAG (with its broad customer base in Berlin) could be integrated into the HEW business in order to make HEW into the required third fully-integrated competitor in the German electricity market. On May 10, considering this new ownership structure of joint control of BEWAG by HEW and Mirant, the FCO, in coordination with the European Commission, approved the overall concept of an acquisition by HEW of VEAG and Laubag.

Deutsche Lufthansa/Eurowings

On September 19, the FCO cleared the acquisition by Deutsche Lufthansa of a 49% share in Eurowings Luftverkehrs AG. The decision is notable for the far-reaching undertakings that were imposed as a condition of approval. Even though the FCO held that the merger would lead to the strengthening of Lufthansa's dominant position on the domestic market for air services, the resulting negative impact

Part II: National Competition Developments

on competition was, in the FCO's view, outweighed by the improvements in market structure brought about by the undertakings. The undertakings are aimed at facilitating the entry of a new competitor, European Air Express (EAE). Toward this end: (i) Lufthansa must open its "Miles & More" program to existing and future competitors; (ii) Lufthansa and Eurowings must transfer some of their domestic air services to EAE, and grant EAE protection from competition for six flight-plan seasons; (iii) Eurowings must sell at least five aircraft to EAE; and (iv) Lufthansa and Eurowings must surrender specified airport take-off and landing slots in the event that EAE decides to expand its flight services.

Sanacorp/Andreae-Noris Zahn

On September 21, the FCO prohibited the proposed acquisition by Sanacorp e.G. of a majority shareholding in Andreae-Noris Zahn AG. These firms are the third- and fourth-largest pharmaceutical wholesalers in Germany, and the combined firm would have had market shares of more than 40% on the regional markets for drug wholesaling in southern Germany and Mecklenburg-Western Pomerania.

Deutsche Post/trans-o-flex Schnell-Lieferdienst

On November 27, the FCO prohibited Deutsche Post AG's acquisition of trans-o-flex Schnell-Lieferdienst GmbH. The FCO held that the merger would have resulted in Deutsche Post having a dominant position in the market for parcel services to business customers and strengthened Deutsche Post's dominant position on the market for mail-order parcel services. The FCO's decision is notable because, on September 27, the FCO had granted the parties an exemption from the normal rule prohibiting consummation of a merger prior to a clearance decision by the FCO or expiry of the relevant waiting periods for clearance.

The FCO's September 27 decision was the first application of Section 41(2) of the Competition Act, which came into effect as of January 1, 1999 and allows the FCO to grant exemptions from the consummation prohibition. A Section 41(2) exemption may be granted for important reasons, in particular to prevent the participating companies or third parties from suffering severe harm as a result of the Act's suspensive effect. In this case, the FCO had granted the exemption so that trans-o-flex could be reorganized and restored to a financially sound position, thereby saving jobs. The FCO had found that if the parties had to await the FCO's decision and any subsequent lawsuits (which could take years) the success of the trans-o-flex reorganization would have been seriously endangered. The exemption had been subject to strict conditions and undertakings. In particular, an extensive duty had been imposed on the companies to inform the FCO about the progress of the reorganization, and Deutsche Post had been ordered to preserve the legal and economic independence of trans-o-flex (under a "hold-separate" order), so that trans-o-flex could be sold to another buyer if the FCO ultimately prohibited the proposed acquisition – as in fact it did on November 27.

BP/Veba Oel; Shell/DEA

On December 19, the FCO cleared the merger of Deutsche BP AG and Veba Oel AG, and the merger of Deutsche Shell GmbH and DEA Mineralöl AG. The BP/Veba Oel and Shell/DEA transactions had been referred by the European Commission to the FCO for merger control examination with respect to their effects on the German downstream markets for oil products. The concentrations were referred under Article 9 of Regulation 4064/89, which allows for referral to a Member State competition authority if a concentration threatens to create or strengthen a dominant position, as a result of which effective competition would be significantly impeded on a distinct market within that Member State. The Commission had found that these conditions had been fulfilled and that the FCO was in the best position to assess the relevant local markets and supply relations in Germany.

The FCO granted clearance subject to strict undertakings that are aimed at ensuring competition in the downstream petroleum markets. Fulfillment of the undertakings will bring the merging companies' aggregate market shares below the threshold of 50%, above which there is a statutory presumption of collective dominance. Shell/DEA and BP/Veba will have to sell 1,500 petrol stations representing 5.3% and 4.0%, respectively, of the total sales volume of domestic petrol stations to third companies. They also undertook to supply fuel to the petrol stations' buyers on favorable terms for up to five years. BP/Veba will also divest its 45% interest in Bayernoil, Germany's largest oil refinery, and Shell/DEA committed itself to offer fuel from its pipeline to competitors on the same terms as an ordinary pipeline operator would.

Promatech/Sulzer

In December, the FCO and the Italian, Spanish, and U.K. competition authorities jointly referred to the European Commission the Italian company Promatech S.p.A.'s proposed acquisition of the Swiss firm Sulzer AG's weaving machines business (see below under Italy, Spain and the United Kingdom). In connection with this matter, the FCO's President, Mr. Böge, commented that he considered the practice of making referrals based on the specific circumstances of individual cases to be preferable to automatic referral in all instances where multiple national filings would otherwise be required. This proposal is currently being discussed in connection with the reform of the EC Merger Regulation.

5.4. POLICY AND PROCEDURE

Electricity Sector Decision Body

The FCO and the cartel authorities of the *Länder* stepped up their efforts to combat abusive practices by electricity network operators. While the European Directive on Electricity of 1996 and the Amended German Energy Act of 1998 created the external framework for competition in the electricity sector, numerous complaints by newcomers entering the electricity market and electricity end-users indicated that there were still obstacles impeding the transition to competition. The main complaint concerns the fees charged by network operators for use of their networks.

In response, the FCO and the *Länder* cartel authorities published a report dated April 19 containing guidelines and common standards for the determination of abusively high network access fees. The report is available on the FCO's website at <www.bundeskartellamt.de>. In the opinion of FCO President Böge, these guidelines and common standards will improve legal security for market participants. However, he also stated that efficient control of network access fees may be difficult, since benchmarking or competitive prices are often not available and the FCO lacks sufficient personnel to monitor network access fees across the country. FCO officials have opposed the European Commission's position that every Member State should have a separate regulatory authority for electricity and gas. Germany is the only Member State without such a separate regulatory authority.

Effective August 1, the FCO set up an 11th Decision Body, which is responsible for the electricity sector. The Decision Body will enforce, in particular, the prohibitions on abuse of a dominant market position through discrimination and refusal of access to networks at adequate network access fees. The Competition Act – and, specifically, the essential facilities provision that was inserted in the Competition Act as of January 1, 1999 – plays an important role in the German energy sector. Germany has opted for a negotiated access system in the electricity and gas sectors, and the sector-specific laws – due to their voluntary character – have arguably been ineffective in establishing real competition on the energy markets. While firms that sought network access and felt unfairly treated could complain to the FCO, it often took too long to obtain an enforceable decision. The new Decision Body has the capacity to hear more cases, instead of limiting itself to a few test cases. As a first major activity, in late September the 11th Decision Body initiated investigating against 22 electricity network operators on suspicion of charging excessive fees for network access.

In an effort to support the FCO in its struggle to establish competition on the energy markets, the Federal government plans to amend the Competition Act to make the FCO's orders in the energy sector, as a rule, immediately enforceable. This proposal is aimed at preventing the established network operators from effectively denying network access by repeatedly appealing the FCO's decisions. The proposal would give the FCO the same authority that sector-specific regulators have, and is thus in accord with Germany's position that no sector-specific energy regulator is required.

6. GREECE

This section reviews developments concerning the Competition Act 703/1977 on the Control of Monopolies and Oligopolies and the Protection of Free Competition (the Competition Act), which is enforced by the National Competition Authority (the Competition Committee), a department of the Ministry of Commerce of Greece.

6.1. VERTICAL RESTRAINTS

Communication on Vertical Agreements

On December 19, the Competition Committee issued a communication on the application of the Competition Act to vertical agreements (*i.e.*, agreements between two or more undertakings, each of which is active at a different level of the production and distribution chain). The Competition Committee decided to adopt the principles introduced by the EC Block Exemption Regulation (Commission Regulation 2790/1999) when considering vertical agreements, including the general principle that the legal treatment of vertical agreements depends on the market share of the supplier (or the buyer, in the case of exclusive supply agreements).

The communication aims at providing guidelines under the Competition Act for vertical agreements that do not fall within the ambit of Article 81(1) EC and cannot therefore benefit from the EC Block Exemption Regulation. These guidelines are based on the criteria set out in the EC Block Exemption Regulation. Thus, the Competition Committee intends to grant "retrospective" exemptions (*i.e.*, exemptions valid as from the date when the agreement was concluded) for vertical agreements that do not satisfy the exemption criteria set out in Article 1(3) of the Competition Act, if: (a) the thresholds provided in Articles 3 and 9 of the EC Block Exemption Regulation are not exceeded in the Greek market; (b) there is no cumulative anti-competitive effect of parallel networks as described in Article 6 of the EC Block Exemption Regulation; and (c) the vertical agreements do not contain restraints such as those described in Articles 4 and 5 of the EC Block Exemption Regulation (which list the categories of agreements types of obligations that may not be exempted).

6. Greece

With regard to the duration of "non-compete obligations" (as defined in Article 1(b) of the EC Block Exemption Regulation) included in vertical agreements, the Competition Committee decided as follows: (a) non-compete obligations that were concluded before May 31, 2000, with a contractual duration terminating by December 31, 2006, fulfil the criteria for the "retroactive" exemption; (b) non-compete obligations concluded before May 31, 2000, that terminate after December 31, 2006, may also be granted an exemption with retroactive effect, until December 31, 2006; and (c) "non-compete obligations" concluded after May 31, 2000, that have a contractual duration of more than five years and do not fall within Article 5(a) of the EC Block Exemption Regulation will be assessed on an individual basis; if they are eligible for an exemption, the Committee will then assess whether it should be granted with retroactive effect. The Greek Competition Committee has jurisdiction to grant exemptions for all agreements except those falling within the ambit of Article 81 EC, exemptions for which may be granted by the European Commission.

6.2. ABUSE OF MARKET POWER

GlaxoWellcome

On August 3, the Competition Committee issued an interim ruling requiring GlaxoWellcome to continue supplying the drugs Imigran, Lamictal, and Severent to pharmacy associations and associations of pharmaceutical wholesalers. In November 2000, GlaxoWellcome had decided to begin selling these products directly to retailers. A number of pharmacy associations and associations of pharmaceutical wholesalers lodged a complaint alleging that GlaxoWellcome was thereby abusing its dominant position in the markets for these products. The complainants also argued that the shortages caused by GlaxoWellcome's quota supply system threatened public health, since there are no substitutes for the three products.

GlaxoWellcome's decision to supply these products directly to pharmacies was based on the fact that, despite increasing demand for these products by certain pharmacy associations and wholesalers, there were still shortages in the Greek market, even though the quantities supplied in that market to the wholesalers and associations exceeded demand. The shortages resulted from intra-Community trade of the products by pharmacy associations and wholesalers. GlaxoWellcome argued that this activity also caused instability in the local markets of other European countries, where pharmacy associations and wholesalers would normally buy the products at higher prices. GlaxoWellcome therefore decided to apply a quota system, according to which it would directly supply pharmacies with quantities of the products slightly higher than those reflected in their actual sales.

In its interim ruling, the Competition Committee held that, until a final decision is made on the case, following the examination of all complaints lodged, GlaxoWellcome should continue to supply the complainants with any quantity of product that they order. Moreover, GlaxoWellcome must continue to supply the products in question to all associations of pharmacies and pharmaceutical wholesalers in Greece in accordance with their orders and not applying any quantitative restrictions. The decision did not reach a final conclusion on whether GlaxoWellcome has abused its dominant position; however, extensive reference was made to the prohibition under EU law of measures, such as the quota system at issue, that may restrict parallel trade. The Competition Committee is expected to issue its final decision by the end of 2002.

7. ITALY

This section reviews developments concerning the Competition Law of October 10, 1990, No 287, which is enforced by the Italian Competition Authority, the decisions of which are appealable to the Regional Administrative Tribunal of Latium.

7.1. HORIZONTAL AGREEMENTS

Otis/Ceam/Kone/Schindler

On January 31, the Tribunal annulled an Authority decision that: (i) Otis/Ceam, Kone, Schindler and 11 other elevator companies, together with *Assoascensori* (the trade association that represents these companies), violated the Competition Law by applying standard contract conditions for elevator sales, and (ii) the three principal operators abused their individual dominant positions in the markets for original spare parts for their own elevators.

The Tribunal noted that the only evidence of an unlawful agreement among the elevator companies was a 1979 document by which they established a common method to calculate prices and price variation. At the time, this clause, drafted to adjust prices to reflect inflation between order and delivery, was lawful since no competition law was in force in Italy. Consequently, the Tribunal stated that, absent other documentary evidence, the Authority had to present detailed proof of the anti-competitive effects of this clause on the market. However, the evidence amassed by the Authority was not sufficient to establish a violation of the Competition Law.

In its decision, the Tribunal also held that the conduct of a dominant firm may be abusive only if such conduct is repeated and generalized. The Authority must prove that the dominant firm possessed a conscious understanding of the impact of its behavior. In the case at issue, the Authority produced evidence of only a single refusal to supply by one of the three companies, which failed to satisfy this burden of proof.

Part II: National Competition Developments

Telecom Italia Mobile/Omnitel Pronto Italia

On March 22, the Supreme Administrative Court (*Consiglio di Stato*) partially annulled a decision of the Authority finding that the two leading Italian mobile telecommunication service providers, Telecom Italia Mobile S.p.A. (TIM) and Omnitel Pronto Italia S.p.A. (OPI), violated the Competition Law by agreeing on (i) the price for fixed-mobile communications in 1998 and 1999; and (ii) the price for interconnection to their mobile networks.

This is the first case in which the Supreme Administrative Court, on the basis of the Court of Justice's case law, outlined the burden of proof that must be satisfied by the Authority in order to show the existence of a concerted practice under the Competition Law. In particular, the Court stated that conscious parallelism among competitors cannot be the only evidence of an agreement or a concerted practice. The Authority must rely on strong and consistent evidence that shows: (i) the absence of alternative plausible explanations of the parallel behavior; or (ii) actual contacts or exchanges of information between the parties. While the burden is on the Authority to prove the absence of alternative explanations for the conduct in question, the parties must prove the lawful purpose of any demonstrated contacts or exchanges of information.

In the case at issue, the Authority's decision was partially quashed because (i) there were several plausible rational explanations for TIM and OPI charging the same tariffs in 1998; and (ii) the parties produced sufficient evidence that their meetings had purposes other than the discussion of the prices for 1998.

Unione Petrolifera

On April 27, the Supreme Administrative Court (*Consiglio di Stato*) annulled a key decision of the Authority in the motor fuel distribution sector. In 2000, the Authority found that the Italian oil companies and their trade association, Unione Petrolifera, violated the Competition Law by carrying out a concerted practice aimed at securing uniform application by gas station managers of the companies' recommended prices.

According to the Authority, one of the main instruments used in this regard was an agreement between Unione Petrolifera and the gas station managers' association on a common method of calculating fuel price discounts offered by oil companies to gas station managers. That agreement, signed in June 1997, was communicated to the Authority by Unione Petrolifera shortly after signing. In its decision, the Supreme Administrative Court found that this communication amounted to a formal notification of an agreement pursuant to the Competition

Law. Under the Competition Law, the Authority has 120 days from a notification to decide whether to open an investigation of the notified agreement. Because the Authority had not acted within this 120-day period, the Court held that the Italian oil companies had a legitimate expectation that their agreement was not anticompetitive. Accordingly, the Court concluded, the Authority could not legitimately declare the agreement in violation of the Competition Law three years after the notification.

After stating that the Authority's procedural inaction was sufficient reason to quash the Authority's decision, the Court also analyzed the appellants' other arguments and found that the Authority had not considered several plausible alternative explanations for the oil companies' parallel behavior. In particular, in the Court's view, the Authority overlooked fundamental peculiarities of the oil sector, where (i) gas station managers have very low profit margins and thus cannot afford to reduce their retail prices significantly; (ii) consumer demand is relatively inelastic and scarcely affected by prices; (iii) recommended prices (not just retail prices) are transparent because their publication is required by regulation; and (iv) competitors were forced by regulation to conclude agreements among themselves on certain subjects.

7.2. ABUSE OF MARKET POWER

Telecom Italia

On April 27, the Authority found that Telecom Italia SpA had abused its dominant position by marketing high-speed internet access products through DSL technology while its competitors were unable to do so due to a lack of required infrastructure. As a result, the Authority imposed on Telecom Italia a fine of approximately ITL 115 billion (€ 59 million). Although not explicitly based on the "essential facilities" doctrine, the Authority's findings were strongly influenced by the position enjoyed by Telecom Italia concerning access to the local loop and the continuing liberalization of this facility provided for by EC Regulation 2887/00.

In reaching its conclusion, the Authority considered that, through ownership of the public switched telecommunications network (PSTN), Telecom Italia enjoyed an advantage not available to its competitors in the supply of DSL services. This is because DSL technology is based on the copper wires that link customer premises to the PSTN (the "local loop") and, therefore, all other operators were dependent on Telecom Italia for the provision of the infrastructure necessary to supply DSL services. Pending the unbundling of the local loop and certain related measures mandated by the Italian Communications Authority (ICA) to ensure competition in the provision of DSL services, the Authority held that Telecom Italia was under an obligation to provide its competitors with an "intermediate product." Accordingly, Telecom Italia's competitors have a right of virtual access to its network under conditions that allow the provision of services to end-users. The Authority found that, by refusing to provide such intermediate product after the ICA's intervention, Telecom Italia had unfairly delayed its provision to competitors.

Alitalia (I)

On June 27, the Authority found that Alitalia Linee Aeree Italiane S.p.A. (Alitalia) abused its dominant position as a purchaser of air travel agency services in Italy. The Authority found that by applying exclusionary incentive schemes, Alitalia foreclosed competitors from the Italian air transport market and discriminated among travel agents. As a result, the Authority fined Alitalia approximately € 27 million. Despite the national dimension of the air travel agency services market, the Authority applied Article 82 EC because Alitalia's abuse also had an impact on trade between Member States. (The Authority's findings closely follow the reasoning of the European Commission in the *Virgin/British Airways* case, which was based on similar facts.)

Alitalia had in place a network of agreements with travel agencies for the sale of Alitalia tickets. To assess the competitive effects of these agreements, the Authority examined the Italian markets for air travel agency and air transport services. According to the Authority, Alitalia's position in the air transport services market made it an indispensable business partner for travel agents. In fact, because sales of Alitalia tickets accounted for a very large proportion of Italian travel agencies' total turnover, no travel agent could decline to offer Alitalia tickets to its customers without incurring major damage to its business. Alitalia was therefore found to enjoy a dominant position as a purchaser in the Italian market for air travel agency services.

The Authority found that, for each travel agent, Alitalia tied commissions to sales targets at a level equal to or higher than its sales of Alitalia tickets in the previous year. Pursuant to established EC case law, the agreements were considered abusive because they gave travel agents an incentive to sell Alitalia tickets rather than those of other airlines, thus foreclosing other airlines from the air transport market. In addition, the Authority found that the incentive schemes were discriminatory because in some cases different commissions were granted to travel agents for reaching similar sales targets. Thus, the agreements placed some travel agents at a competitive disadvantage relative to the others without an acceptable justification.

Alitalia (II)

On November 14, the Authority found that Alitalia Linee Aeree Italiane S.p.A. (Alitalia) did not abuse its dominant position in the route between Milan and Lamezia Terme (in Southern Italy) by charging excessive fares. The investigation had begun as a result of numerous complaints from passengers, consumers' associations, and local authorities that fares on this route were unjustifiably higher than those charged on the comparable Milan–Reggio Calabria route.

The Authority's decision is interesting because it illustrates the methodology that the Authority follows to establish whether the prices charged by a company holding a dominant position may be considered excessive. The Authority's analysis proceeded in two stages. First, it compared the conditions offered by Alitalia on the relevant route with those available on a comparable route where Alitalia was subject to competitive constraints (Milan–Reggio Calabria). This comparison showed that Alitalia's revenue per passenger on the Milan–Lamezia Terme route was more than 50% higher than the revenue per passenger on the comparable route. However, the Authority noted that Alitalia always reported significant losses on the Milan–Reggio Calabria route and, thus, the fares charged on this route did not constitute a valid benchmark to assess the fairness of the prices on the dominated market.

Second, the Authority compared Alitalia's return per passenger on the relevant route with the cost of offering the service. The Authority did not consider that Alitalia's profit margin on the route of 32% in 1999 and 31% in 2000 indicated clearly any unreasonable disproportion between the price and the commercial value of the service provided. In conclusion, the Authority held that the evidence was not sufficient to demonstrate that Alitalia's pricing policies on the Milan–Lamezia Terme route constituted an abuse of a dominant position.

7.3. MERGERS AND ACQUISITIONS

Seat Pagine Gialle/Cecchi Gori Communications

On January 23, the Authority conditionally approved the acquisition by Seat Pagine Gialle SpA, a subsidiary of Telecom Italia, of sole control of Cecchi Gori Communications SpA. Despite the approval, the transaction could not be completed immediately because, on January 19, the Italian Communications Authority (ICA) declared it incompatible with applicable regulations on the telecommunication, radio, and television sectors.

Part II: National Competition Developments

Article 4(8) of Law No 249/97 prohibits the "exclusive licensee" for the provision of public telecommunication services from being active at the same time in radio or television broadcasting. According to the ICA, although Telecom Italia is no longer an "exclusive licensee" following the liberalization of the telecommunications market, it still enjoys a quasi-monopolistic position, and the prohibition should therefore have continued to apply.

On appeal, however, the Tribunal annulled the ICA's decision by holding that Telecom Italia could no longer be considered an "exclusive licensee" and, therefore, Article 4(8) no longer applied to the company. The Tribunal also noted that, in assessing the impact of mergers, the Authority should play a more important role than the ICA.

The Tribunal's judgment was affirmed by the Supreme Administrative Court. Therefore, Seat Pagine Gialle's acquisition of Cecchi Gori was completed, subject to certain conditions imposed by the Authority to prevent the strengthening of Telecom Italia's dominant position in the markets for internet access services, the collection of advertising for telephone and business directories, and the collection of online advertising. The most important of these conditions is that Telecom Italia must allow its competitors access on a non-discriminatory basis to all of its infrastructure for the deployment of fiber optic cable.

Granarolo/Centrale del Latte di Vicenza

On May 24, the Authority prohibited Granarolo SpA's planned acquisition of Centrale del Latte di Vicenza SpA, a milk and milk products producer and distributor, and one of the strongest remaining competitors, in the Veneto region. The Authority found that the acquisition would have created a collectively dominant position involving Granarolo and Parmalat in the Veneto fresh milk market.

This is the first case in which the Authority has found that a transaction would create a collectively dominant position. As a result of the transaction, Granarolo would have increased its 15-18% market share to 25-28%, close to that of its main competitor Parmalat (30-33%). Thus, the combined market shares of the two main players on the Veneto fresh milk market could have been nearly 60%. In addition to market shares, the Authority took into account for the third time in its 10-year history the level of concentration in the market, as shown by the Herfindal-Hirschman Index (HHI). (It is notable that the Bank of Italy refers regularly to HHI levels in its review of bank mergers.) The Authority held that a 326-point increase in the HHI was excessive because, pursuant to the U.S. Merger guidelines, an increase by more than 100 points in similar situations is likely to produce restrictive effects on competition.

In addition to examining market concentration, the Authority noted that the market is characterized by the following features indicating that the market is susceptible to oligopolistic behavior: (i) stagnating milk consumption and low likelihood of market growth; (ii) product homogeneity; (iii) technology that is not subject to significant improvement; (iv) producers that share the same cost structures; (v) high barriers to market entry and a low probability of new market entrants; and (vi) transparent prices. Finally, the Authority noted that both Granarolo and Parmalat had followed the same strategy of acquisitions throughout Italy. Consequently, according to the Authority, economic interdependence between the two players in several geographic markets creates a strong disincentive for the adoption of aggressive pricing policies in each single market, since an action by one of them aimed at gaining market shares in one market could be "punished" through retaliatory measures in another market.

This situation could have led to a tacit convergence in the market conduct of Granarolo and Parmalat, which would have been able to act independently of their competitors and consumers. Local milk producers in the Veneto would have been too weak to compete effectively with Granarolo and Parmalat and would have been forced to accept their pricing policies.

Enel/France Télécom/Infostrada

On November 14, the Tribunal annulled the Authority's decision conditionally authorizing the acquisition by Enel S.p.A. and France Télécom SA of joint control of the Italian telecommunications operator Infostrada S.p.A. In its decision, the Authority had stated that Enel enjoyed a dominant position in the markets for both electricity generation and electricity sale, and found that the acquisition of Infostrada would enable Enel to become a multi-utility company and, thus, to capture the loyalty of electricity customers by its ability to bundle telecommunications services with electricity. Therefore, to promote competition on the electricity market, the Authority had made the acquisition subject to the divestiture of at least 5,500 MW of Enel's generating capacity (an amount equal to the current aggregate generating capacity of Enel's competitors).

The Tribunal annulled the Authority's decision because it found that Enel did not hold a dominant position in the market for the sale of electricity, and, therefore, no divestiture of generating capacity was needed. According to the Tribunal, the Authority's analysis failed to take into account the recent decrease in Enel's market share (approximately from 90% to 50%). Over an 18-month period following liberalization of the electricity sector, Enel lost about 40% of the Italian electricity market to new entrants, demonstrating that (i) Enel was not able to act inde-

Part II: National Competition Developments

pendently of its customers and competitors; and (ii) the market was characterized by lively competition, capable of taking advantage of any dissatisfaction on the part of Enel's customers.

Promatech/Sulzer

On December 18, the competition authorities of Germany, Italy, Spain and the United Kingdom jointly requested the European Commission to consider the Italian company Promatech S.p.A.'s proposed acquisition of the Swiss firm Sulzer AG's textile business (see above under Germany and below under Spain and the United Kingdom). The request was made under Article 22(3) of the EC Merger Regulation, which allows Member States to refer a merger proposal to the Commission, even if it does not meet the thresholds of the EC Merger Regulation. This is the first occasion on which a number of Member States have acted together to make such a request. It is intended that the European Commission will, as a result, be able to carry out a single, coordinated investigation of the transaction's impact on competition in all the Member States concerned. Recent improvements in communications between the national competition authorities enabled the necessary coordination to take place within the deadlines set out in Article 22 of the EC Merger Regulation.

7.4. POLICY AND PROCEDURE

Amendments to Competition Law

On March 5, the Italian Parliament amended the Competition Law to provide that a firm entrusted with the operation of services of general economic interest can operate in other markets only through a separate entity, the formation of which must be communicated to the Authority. Further, if the firm performing services of general interest provides its controlled companies with goods or services, it must make such goods and services available to its subsidiaries' direct competitors on equivalent terms. The Authority has the power to impose fines for violations of the new rules.

In order to give more discretion to the Authority in setting the fines for substantive violations of the Competition Law, the Parliament also modified the Competition Law to allow the Authority to issue fines of up to 10% of the world-wide turnover of a firm that participates in an anti-competitive agreement or abuses its dominant position. As a result, in calculating fines, the Authority is no longer bound to consider only the turnover derived from the activities that are the subject matter of the agreement or the abuse. In addition, the previous one percent minimum for fines was eliminated. By giving the Authority this power to impose merely symbolic fines, the Parliament hopes to encourage whistle-blowing.

New Merger Notification Thresholds

On April 24, the Authority established new turnover thresholds triggering the obligation to notify concentrations, namely: (i) combined aggregate turnover of the parties in Italy (net of indirect taxes and sales rebates) of ITL 730 billion (€ 377 million); or (ii) turnover in Italy by the target company or business of ITL 73 billion (€ 37 million).

8. THE NETHERLANDS

This section reviews developments concerning the Competition Act of January 1, 1998, which is enforced by the Dutch Competition Authority.

8.1. POLICY AND PROCEDURE

Change in Competition Authority Status

On March 19, the Minister of Economic Affairs proposed a draft bill by which the Competition Authority will obtain the status of an independent governmental agency (*zelfstandig bestuursorgaan*).

Currently, the Authority operates under the direct supervision of the Minister of Economic Affairs. The Minister has the authority to instruct the Authority, both generally and in individual cases. The authority to give general instructions is understood to allow the Minister to instruct the Authority to change its enforcement policies and priorities. In addition, the Minister currently has the right to "overrule" the Authority's final refusal to clear a concentration if the Minister considers that the general interest outweighs the transaction's restrictions on competition. The Minister has never availed himself of these powers.

Under the proposal, the Minister would no longer have the authority to instruct the Authority in individual cases involving purely national matters. However, the Minister would retain the authority to instruct the Authority in individual international cases and the right to "overrule" the Authority's final refusal to clear a concentration if the Minister considers that the general interest outweighs the transaction's restrictions on competition. The proposal would also grant the Minister authority to have the Authority enforce European or other competition rules, including those contained in treaties or international agreements, to the extent not already provided for in the Competition Act. The explanatory memorandum states that, in cases affecting the Netherlands as a Member State, the Minister must retain ultimate responsibility.

Competition Authority 2000 Annual Report

In April 2001, the Competition Authority published its annual report for the year 2000. The report notes that (i) the Authority's tasks and responsibilities expanded and will continue to expand in the near future (*e.g.*, in the areas of local and regional public bus transportation, railroads, and competition between public and private entities); (ii) the Authority responded to most of the exemption requests from the ban on restrictive agreements filed with the Authority once the Competition Act came into force; (iii) the number of merger notifications received by the Authority increased to 197 in 2000 (up from 140 in 1999); and (iv) the Authority has started to take a more proactive stance in the enforcement of the Competition Act.

The report further notes that: (i) the Authority will allocate more staff for *ex officio* investigations and the handling of complaints; (ii) the Authority will continue to consider introduction of a leniency notice (note that the Director-General stated in December 2000 that adoption of such a policy would occur in the spring of 2001); and (iii) the Authority has requested that the Minister of Economic Affairs increase merger notification thresholds (see next item below). The report also concludes that the current level of fines for failure to await merger clearance before consummation of a notifiable transaction (NLG 50,000, or € 23,000), and failure to cooperate or provide complete and correct information (NLG 10,000, or € 4,500), are too low to provide a sufficient deterrent in all cases.

New Merger Notification Thresholds

On September 28, the Minister of Economic Affairs increased the national turnover threshold for merger control review from approximately € 13.6 million to € 30 million. The increase came into effect on October 17. The threshold for the total consolidated (worldwide) turnover of all undertakings concerned in a relevant transaction (€ 113,450,000) and the thresholds applicable to credit and financial institutions and insurers remain unchanged.

Transactions that do not involve credit and financial institutions or insurers are now notifiable in the Netherlands only if at least two of the undertakings concerned have individual turnovers in the Netherlands exceeding € 30 million and all the undertakings concerned have a combined worldwide turnover exceeding € 113,450,000.

This increase is expected to reduce the administrative burden on small- and medium-sized companies and to result in 50 to 75 fewer notifiable transactions per year. The Authority is thus expected to deploy more of its resources toward in-depth investigations and larger transactions.

The Minister of Economic Affairs also stated that a market share jurisdictional threshold in addition to the turnover test would be considered. Such a test could result in some transactions being notifiable even though the turnover thresholds are not exceeded. The introduction of such a market share test would require an amendment to the Competition Act.

Fining Guidelines

On December 19, the Competition Authority published its first guidelines on the method of setting fines for anti-competitive practices and abuses of dominant positions. The method begins from a base amount, which is multiplied by a factor for "gravity of the infringement" and then adjusted upward or downward based on various aggravating and mitigating circumstances.

The base amount is set at 10% of the aggregate turnover realized by the undertaking involved through the sale of the relevant goods or services during the term of the infringement. Alternate methods of calculating the base amount may apply in special cases, such as "bid-rigging" and cases involving trade associations.

The base amount will then be multiplied by a factor intended to represent the gravity of the infringement. In case of "very serious infringements" (*e.g.*, horizontal restrictions with respect to price and/or quantity and exclusionary practices by dominant entities), this factor will be between 1.5 and 3.0. In case of "serious infringements" (*e.g.*, other horizontal restrictions), the factor will not exceed 2.0. In case of "less serious infringements" (*e.g.*, vertical restrictions with a limited market impact and not affecting price or quantity), the factor will not exceed 1.0.

The resulting amount can then be increased or decreased in order to take account of the "economic context" in which the infringements occurred, the total turnover of the undertaking realized in the Netherlands, and a number of specified aggravating and mitigating circumstances similar to those developed by the European Commission under its fining practice. Unlike the European Commission, the Authority considers the payment of compensatory damages by the undertaking involved, on its own initiative, to be a mitigating circumstance.

Finally, the Authority announced that it intends to publish draft leniency guidelines in the near future.

9. SPAIN

This section reviews developments concerning the Law for the Protection of Competition of 1989, which is enforced by the Tribunal for the Protection of Competition and the Service for the Protection of Competition.

9.1. VERTICAL RESTRAINTS

La Casera

The Tribunal extended for an additional five years the exemption granted on May 23, 1996 to La Casera (a soft drinks manufacturer in Spain) on its Franchising and Exclusive Distribution Standard Agreement. The Agreement, among other things, imposes on La Casera's distributors an obligation to communicate to La Casera information regarding passive sales performed outside their assigned distribution territories. In 1996, the Tribunal held that this restriction did not contravene Article 3.3(a) of EC Regulation 240/96, which prohibits restrictions on passive sales. In granting the exemption the Tribunal found that relevant circumstances justifying the initial exemption persist.

9.2. HORIZONTAL AGREEMENTS

Madrid Airport Cargo Operators

The Tribunal fined the Madrid Airport Local Cargo Airport Operation Committee (AOC), which is composed of a group of major European and non-European airlines, PTA 12 million (€ 72,121) for concluding a restrictive agreement prohibited by Article 1 of the Competition Law.

Airport authorities charge an "E-2 fee" to airport cargo operators (including the AOC members) for administrative expenses. The AOC members agreed uniformly and simultaneously to pass the E-2 fee through to end-users of their services. The defendants offered three main arguments as justification for this conduct, all of which were rejected by the Tribunal.

First, according to the defendants, the transfer of the fee was permissible under Law 25/1998, Budget Law of the Comunidad *Autónoma de Madrid*, which allows cargo operators to pass the E-2 fee through to their customers. The Tribunal, however, found that while the law might entitle individual firms to pass the fee through to end-users, it does not authorize a collective arrangement to do so; a uniform transfer of this fee would substantially restrict competition among cargo operators, in violation of Article 1 of the Competition Law.

Second, the defendants argued that the E-2 fee pass-through was a mere recommendation and not an agreement. The Tribunal rejected this defense, stating that any collective recommendation that can impede, restrict or distort competition in all or part of the national market is expressly prohibited under Article 1.

Third, the defendants argued that the pass-through arrangement was of *de minimis* effect. The Tribunal also rejected this defense, stating that, regardless of the quantitative impact of the conduct in question, the use of a collective organization for the achievement of illegal collusive purposes should be strictly condemned. (Note that there is no *de minimis* exception for Article 1 violations.)

Dairy Cartel

In an important judgment, the High Administrative Court (*Audiencia Nacional*) dismissed an appeal by a number of Spanish milk producers against the Tribunal's decision finding illegal cartel behavior and upheld the fines imposed by the Tribunal, on December 14 (almost four years after the defendants appealed the fines).

This case is particularly interesting because the Tribunal cited no direct evidence of a price-fixing agreement, illegal information exchange, or collusion among the parties. Unlike EU competition laws, Spanish law extends the prohibition on cartel behavior to conduct amounting to "conscious parallelism" as a more sophisticated form of illegal "concerted practice." The companies based their defense on an "oligopolistic interdependence" argument derived from classic oligopoly pricing theory (more specifically, on the "barometric price leadership" doctrine, which holds that competitors set their prices based on those of the market leader).

The Court's judgment reveals a disappointing lack of economic analysis of this highly complex case. Such decisions have fueled a growing debate in Spain as to whether administrative courts (which are responsible for a wide range of issues outside the realm of competition law) are properly equipped to handle competition cases involving technical economic arguments. In response, there have been a number of proposals directed at creating specialized sections in the Spanish judicial system to deal with competition cases.

9.3. ABUSE OF MARKET POWER

Telefónica Móviles

Distribuciones Mob, S.A. submitted a claim against Telefónica Móviles, S.A. for alleged abuse of a dominant position in breach of Article 6 of the Competition Law. In its investigation, the Tribunal found that Telefónica Móviles had included a group of telephone distribution companies (including the complainant) on a "black list," impeding their ability to distribute mobile telephones. The Tribunal also determined that Telefónica Móviles had abused its dominant position by exercising pressure on wholesale suppliers to impede the activities of the companies on the list. The Tribunal fined Telefónica Móviles PTA 50 million (€ 300,000).

Cepsa/Repsol

In one month, the Tribunal ruled on two similar claims against oil companies, with differing results. In the first case, the Asociación de Propietarios de Estaciones de Servicio y Unidades de Suministro de Andalucía (Association of Gas Station Owners and Supply Units of Andalucía) claimed that Compañía Española de Petróleos, S.A. and Cepsa Estaciones de Servicio, S.A. (together, Cepsa) had engaged in restrictive practices relating to exclusive distribution of oil products, in violation of Article 1 of the Competition Law. According to the Association, Cepsa infringed EC Regulation 84/83 by imposing *de facto* exclusive purchase obligations on its distributors through various mechanisms involving real estate rights, cross-lease contracts, credits, fixing prices and commercial margins, and establishing "best price" ("most favored nation") clauses. Following its investigation, the Tribunal found that Cepsa had breached Article 1 by fixing distributors' prices under a regime of agency or commission contracts not protected by Regulation 84/83. The Tribunal fined Cepsa PTA 200 million (€ 1.2 million).

In the second case, the gas station Arenas Camacho, S.L. alleged that Repsol Comercial de Productos Petrolíferos, S.A. had engaged in prohibited conduct under EC Regulation 84/83. In this case, Arenas claimed that in the context of their commercial relationship (exclusive distribution), Repsol breached the regulation by: (i) selling directly to its gas station clients; (ii) imposing an exclusive purchase obligation by means of contract; (iii) reserving certain privileges related to publicity beyond what the regulation allows; and (iv) concealing the contract's real duration, which was over the 10 years permitted by the regulation. The Tribunal rejected this claim on the basis of lack of evidence of the alleged infringements.

Part II: National Competition Developments

Empresa Mixta de Servicios Funerarios de Madrid

The Tribunal fined Empresa Mixta de Servicios Funerarios de Madrid, S.A. (EMSFM) PTA 12 million (€ 72,121) for the abuse of a dominant position in breach of Article 6 of the Competition Law. The Tribunal identified three markets where EMSFM is active: funerary services, graveyard services and residue elimination services. EMSFM holds a statutory monopoly for graveyard services and residue elimination services, but competes against private companies in the provision of funerary services. The Tribunal found that EMSFM had abused its dominant position in the graveyard services market by offering favorable service and pricing terms for graveyard services to families who also acquired funerary services from EMSFM. This discrimination also indirectly prejudiced private companies that offered competing funerary services.

9.4. MERGERS AND ACQUISITIONS

Endesa/Iberdrola

Endesa and Iberdrola, Spain's leading domestic power companies, abandoned their merger plans in February, partly because the undertakings imposed by the government in its final decision to approve the transaction, though less stringent than those initially recommended by the Tribunal, were too onerous.

The government's approval was conditioned on several measures. First, the merged entity would have had to reduce its share of the electricity generation market from just under 80% to no more than 42%. As an interim measure, the merged company would have been allowed to retain 61% of generation assets through a transition period expiring in 2005, but the additional 19% of assets would have had to be managed by an independent holding company. Second, in the distribution market, where the parties' combined market share is about 60%, the combined group would have been allowed to own no more than 48% of national distribution assets. Third, the parties' combined share of the electricity supply market would have been limited to 40%, except in those areas where both Endesa and Iberdrola currently have supply activities, where the cap would have been 60%. Fourth, the government required restrictions on the stakes that the combined group would have been allowed to hold in other energy companies. In addition to these undertakings, the government would have retained the power to intervene and alter the timetable or other procedures related to the required divestitures.

The transaction would also have meant a significant reduction in the amount of state aid granted to the companies for making the transition to a free market, because the calculation for determining such aid had been amended to make it compatible with EU legislation.

Pio Coronado/Cemetro

The Tribunal approved with undertakings the acquisition of Cemetro, S.L. by Pio Coronado, S.A. (part of the Dutch Group Ahold). Both companies are active in the commercial food distribution sector. According to the Tribunal, the relevant markets affected by the transaction were: (i) the local market for retail distribution of goods for daily consumption; (ii) the regional market for wholesale distribution of "cash & carry" goods for daily consumption; and (iii) the national (if not larger) market for storage of goods for daily consumption.

The Tribunal found that the transaction could impede effective competition at the local and regional levels. Nonetheless, it authorized the transaction subject to the divestiture of Cemetro's businesses in two Spanish towns: Los Corales and Mogán. The Tribunal further held that the Service should monitor Pio Coronado's commercial conduct while Cemetro retained ownership of the two stores to be divested. The Council of Ministers later authorized the transaction and imposed undertakings coinciding with those proposed by the Tribunal.

Nutreco España/Agrovic Alimentación

The Tribunal approved with undertakings the acquisition by Nutreco España, S.A. (wholly owned by Nutreco France, S.A.) of Agrovic Alimentación, S.A (wholly owned by Montmelley, S.A.). The relevant markets were: (i) production and sale of live chickens; (ii) chicken for distribution in the *horeca* channel; (iii) chicken for distribution through modern channels (iv) chicken for distribution through traditional channels; (v) chicken for distribution among industrial suppliers; (vi) manufacture and sale of foodstuffs; and (vii) manufacture of corrective products for foodstuffs. The Tribunal considered markets (vi) and (vii) to be national in scope, with the rest having both national and international dimensions. The Tribunal found that the transaction did not result in excessive concentration in any of these markets.

The Tribunal did, however, have questions regarding the fixing of reference prices for live chickens distributed through traditional channels. It found that such prices are fixed on Fridays, by vote of the Lonja Agropecuaria del Ebro (Commercial Association of Growers), made up of growers and industrial suppliers (*i.e.*, slaughterhouses). Nutreco España held 22% of the votes in this association and Agrovic held an additional 24%, so that the merged entity would have held 46% of

Part II: National Competition Developments

the votes. The Tribunal objected to this concentration and recommended not allowing Nutreco España to increase its voting power beyond the 22% that it already held. The price-fixing mechanism of this association remains subject to further review by the Tribunal.

The Council of Ministers later authorized the transaction, but subject to undertakings different from those proposed by the Tribunal. The Council of Ministers ordered that Nutreco España should report to the Service for three years the following detailed information: (i) weekly quantities and prices imposed by Nutreco Group in its sales of both live and slaughtered chickens, broken down by distribution channel; and (ii) analyses of price evolution in the reference prices set by the Lonja Agropecuaria del Ebro every three months.

Iberdrola Redes

On December 21, the Spanish Cabinet prohibited the acquisition by Iberdrola Redes (a subsidiary of one of Spain's leading domestic power companies) of three regional electricity distribution companies (Berrieza, Serviliano García, and Afrodisio Pascual). In so doing, it endorsed the advice given by the Tribunal.

Although the three target companies held very small shares of the relevant markets, the Government and Tribunal each highlighted the importance of preserving independent distribution companies to ensure transparency and efficient operation of pricing mechanisms. They also reasoned that allowing further vertical integration in the electricity sector would run counter to the utility regulatory framework, which requires separation of electricity generation and distribution activities.

This case follows the Government's May, 2000 prohibition of the Unión Fenosa/Hidrocantábrico transaction and the burdensome undertakings imposed on the Endesa/Iberdrola transaction that caused the parties to abandon the deal. It underscores the Government's position that, in such highly concentrated markets with oligopolistic structures, even small increases in market share are likely to raise major antitrust concerns.

Promatech/Sulzer

In December, the German, Italian, Spanish, and U.K. competition authorities jointly referred to the European Commission the Italian company Promatech S.p.A.'s proposed acquisition of the Swiss firm Sulzer AG's weaving machines business (see above under Germany and Italy and below under the United Kingdom).

9.5. JOINT VENTURES

Terra Networks/Banco Bilbao Vizcaya Argentaria

The Tribunal granted an exemption to Terra Networks, S.A. and Banco Bilbao Vizcaya Argentaria S.A. (BBVA) in relation to an agreement concerning the development and establishment of an internet banking venture through UNOE Bank, S.A., a BBVA subsidiary. Under the agreement, Terra would acquire 49% of UNOE. Terra, which is part of the Telefónica Group, is one of the largest Spanish internet and e-commerce firms. BBVA is one of Spain's largest banks.

The Tribunal considered that the agreement did not amount to a merger, as it did not result in joint control over UNOE. According to the Tribunal, despite Terra's large minority shareholding, UNOE's strategic and commercial policy would remain exclusively in the hands of BBVA. Accordingly, the agreement was analyzed under Article 1 of the Competition Law and Article 81 EC.

The Tribunal cited four main reasons for granting the exemption: (i) although they were potential competitors in the relevant market for internet banking, Terra and BBVA were not actual competitors; (ii) the risk that the venture could restrict competition in this market was outweighed by the pro-competitive benefits to result from the creation of a "financial supermarket," such as improved market transparency and greater access to the offered services; (iii) because UNOE's current activity in the relevant market is limited, the venture would not increase Terra's market power as an internet portal or as an e-commerce company; and (iv) the agreement did not restrict the parties' ability to compete independently in the markets to be served by the joint venture. Consequently, the Tribunal determined that the transaction did not constitute a restrictive agreement under Article 1 of the Competition Law or Article 81 EC.

9.6. POLICY AND PROCEDURE

Draft Regulation on Agreements Qualifying for EC Block Exemptions

A draft regulation was proposed that would authorise all agreements that affect the national market and fall under any of the current EC block exemption regulations (*i.e.*, vertical restraints, technology transfer agreements, specialization agreements, and R&D agreements). With respect to the procedure for gaining such authorization, the most relevant features of the draft regulation are that: (i) the agreement should be presented in Spanish (or translated into Spanish from the original language); (ii) if various companies or associations participate in the agreement, a

Part II: National Competition Developments

single notification should be submitted (either subscribed to by, or provided to, all participants); (iii) the parties may submit all the information they consider necessary for assessment of the agreement; (iv) a hearing can be requested; and (v) within a maximum period of 30 days, the Service must refer the case, and recommend a decision, to the Tribunal. Proceedings before the Tribunal may last from approximately 10 days up to three months.

Draft Law regarding Regional Competition Authorities [116]

In 1999, the Spanish Constitutional Court determined that the Constitution does not assign the preservation of competition exclusively to the national government. As a result, certain Autonomous Regions competent in internal trade matters may also exercise competency in competition matters. Article 1 of the new law proposes that the national government would be competent to investigate cases where restrictive conduct threatens competition at a national or broader level. Autonomous Regions with competency in competition matters may be entitled to exercise control over cases of restrictive conduct and individual authorizations where the effects do not spill over from their area of competency. Nonetheless, control of concentrations and state aid, together with the application of block exemptions, will always remain within the competency of the national government. Article 3 of the draft proposes the creation of a Consultative Committee (*Junta Consultiva*) in the event of a conflict of competencies between the national government and the Autonomous Regions or between one Autonomous Region and another. This Committee may resort for assistance to the Tribunal. Article 5 proposes the creation of the Council for the Defense of Competition, which would be in charge of collaboration, coordination and transfer of information between the national government and the Autonomous Regions to foster the uniform application of competition laws. The Autonomous Regions will be obliged to inform the Service of cases being dealt with by their respective competition authorities.

OECD Recommendation on Tribunal

The OECD report on Spain recommends that Spain strengthen the Tribunal by increasing its political independence (the Tribunal is presently composed of

---

[116] A law regarding the competition enforcement competence of the autonomous regions was ultimately enacted on February 21, 2002 (Law 1/2002).

government-designated members and is not perceived as independent from the government). The OECD report also warns of the power of electricity companies and recommends that Spain take measures to increase competition in the markets for electricity generation and distribution. In its first reaction to this report, the government announced its willingness to increase the independence and expand the resources of the Tribunal.

Amendments to Competition Law

The Competition Law has been amended in an effort to increase the Tribunal's independence, financial autonomy and budget. Among the key financial changes is a provision that the Tribunal will receive 50% of the revenue derived from a new pre-merger filing fee. It is hoped that this will allow the Tribunal to increase its staff. This independent source of funding could to some extent insulate the Tribunal from political influence, although the Tribunal remains significantly dependent upon the Ministry of Economy (which is responsible for supervising the Tribunal's "efficiency"). Moreover, the eight members of the Tribunal and its Chairperson remain appointees of the Minister of Economy, which selects the group from "lawyers, economists and other professionals of established reputation."

With these new provisions, the Government seems to have partially followed the OECD recommendation stressing the need for Spain to increase the political independence of the Tribunal; nevertheless, the appointment system ensures that it will remain composed of government-designated members.

The Competition Law now also prescribes the filing fees that must accompany the mandatory merger notification form (figures presented here are approximate): (i) € 3,000 if the parties' combined turnover in Spain is less than € 240 million; (ii) € 6,000 if the parties' combined turnover in Spain is between € 240 million and € 480 million; (iii) € 12,000 if the parties' combined turnover in Spain is between € 480 million and € 3 billion; and (iv) if the parties' combined turnover in Spain exceeds € 3 billion, a flat amount of € 24,000 plus an additional € 6,000 for each additional € 3 billion in combined turnover, to a maximum of € 60,000. There is no variation in the filing fee based on the size of the transaction, which means that large firms entering into even small transactions that are notifiable in Spain will pay very high notification fees.

Decree on Merger Control Procedure

After a lengthy consultation process, the Spanish Government has finally approved Royal Decree 1443/2001 of December 21, 2001, which elaborates on the merger control rules and procedural provisions laid out in the Competition Law. The new statute repeals Decree 1080/1992, and was badly needed, as Spanish merger control regulations have gradually moved from a voluntary, post-transaction review system to a mandatory, pre-transaction suspensive system. The decree also introduces a number of changes resulting from practical experience accumulated by the Service and Tribunal, which should result in a more user-friendly and predictable system.

The Decree includes three main elements. First, it clarifies and develops certain provisions regarding the calculation of turnover and the concept of control, which are intended to harmonize these provisions with the EU Merger Regulation. Control is now defined as the potential to "exercise a decisive influence" over another company's activities.

Second, the Decree establishes the procedural rules to be followed by the Spanish competition authorities under the new system of compulsory pre-transaction notification of mergers. It provides for a possible termination of proceedings during the first phase of a merger investigation, at the discretion of the Minister of Economy. In cases where competition issues can easily be remedied, the Minister can give the parties an opportunity to offer undertakings or make changes to the transaction that would eliminate or reduce the identified competition issues.

Third, the Decree includes the standard notification form to be filed by merging parties. The form seems to retain the EU's former distinction between cooperative and concentrative joint-ventures, instead of replicating the new EU distinction between full-function and non-full-function joint ventures.

It remains unclear what event triggers the obligation to file: the Decree merely indicates that the filing can be made as soon as there is a "project" to acquire or merge, even if the relevant agreement is subject to the fulfillment of conditions precedent. Moreover, unlike the EU system (but like, for example, the U.S. system), there is no specified deadline by which a filing must be made, although reportable transactions cannot be implemented until clearance is received.

Royal Decree 1443/2001 also clarifies merger control procedures in the context of takeover bids. Under the new system, if a takeover triggers Spanish merger control rules, the bidder must give notification of the transaction within five days of filing its prospectus with the Spanish Securities Commission.

The new statute also deals with the implications of various merger control scenarios on the takeover bid. If the Service refers a case to the Tribunal for further review, the bidder is entitled to withdraw its bid. However, if the bidder decides to continue with the takeover and the Ministry of Economy does not lift the suspension, the bid will be deemed conditional on regulatory approval, and the acceptance period for the target company's shareholders will be extended until the Government tacitly or expressly approves the transaction. These provisions will have the following consequences: (i) if the Government does not oppose the merger, the bid will be given full effect; (ii) if the Government blocks the merger, the bidder will be forced to withdraw the bid; and (iii) if the Government clears the transaction subject to conditions, the bidder will have the right to decide whether it prefers to proceed and meet such conditions or to withdraw the bid.

10. SWEDEN

This section reviews developments concerning the Competition Act of 1993, which is enforced by the Competition Authority. Appeals from its decisions to prohibit mergers or acquisitions are heard by the Stockholm District Court.

10.1. HORIZONTAL AGREEMENTS

Uponor/Aktiebolaget Svenska Wavin/KWH PIPE Sverige

The Stockholm District Court found that the companies Uponor AB, Aktiebolaget Svenska Wavin and KWH PIPE Sverige AB infringed Article 6 of the Competition Act. The companies, which are active in the market for plastic sewage pipes, were found, among other things, to have engaged in market allocation and price-fixing for a period of several years. The Court imposed a fine of SEK 10.6 million (€ 1.18 million), which is the highest ever in a Swedish cartel case.

10.2. ABUSE OF MARKET POWER

Scandinavian Airline System

The Market Court (the supreme competition court) affirmed the Competition Authority's decision finding that implementation by Scandinavian Airline System (SAS) of its EuroBonus frequent flyer program on domestic Swedish flights constitutes an abuse of a dominant position. In doing so, the Court severely restricted SAS's ability to offer frequent flyer points on domestic Swedish flights. (The use of EuroBonus on international flights was not part of the case.)

EuroBonus awards bonus points to individual travelers when travelling with SAS and cooperating airline companies, regardless of whether the traveler or the traveler's employer pays for the ticket. The bonus points may then be used to pay for, *e.g.*, flights and hotel rooms.

In defining the relevant market, the Court upheld the Competition Authority's view that the relevant market is the market for "regular air transport of passengers in Sweden." SAS had submitted that relevant markets should be defined as specific routes in Sweden. However, the Court observed that SAS's bonus program was used on all flights in Sweden and that travelers' employers, which often pay for the flights, often conclude agreements with SAS covering all domestic flights. Finally, SAS's behavior affects the entire Swedish aviation market. As a result, the Court concluded that defining relevant markets on a point-to-point basis was not appropriate. The Court then upheld the Authority's view that SAS held a dominant position on the relevant market, accounting for about 75% of domestic Swedish flights.

The Court proceeded to examine whether SAS had abused this dominant position through its use of EuroBonus. The Court found that the structural conditions on the Swedish domestic market limit the possibilities for competition and that EuroBonus discourages new entry and makes it difficult for airlines that do not participate in the program to attract customers. The Court's investigation showed that, in significant part as a result of loyalties created by EuroBonus, even significant discounts offered by SAS's competitors generally did not result in the attraction of new passengers. As a result, the Court concluded that SAS's use of EuroBonus constituted an abuse of a dominant position.

In its defense, SAS explained that its competitors on the Swedish market were allowed to participate in EuroBonus. The Court found this inadequate, however, because this would have forced SAS's competitors to leave other frequent flyer programs and would have given SAS access to confidential information about the competitors' passengers.

The Court found that the only way to eliminate EuroBonus's exclusionary effects was to prohibit SAS from offering EuroBonus points for domestic flights. This prohibition was limited to flights on routes where SAS and/or its cooperating airline partners face competition or potential competition from other airlines. (Some routes in Sweden cannot sustain more than one carrier and the exclusionary effect of EuroBonus would not be felt there.)

The prohibition was combined with a fine of SEK 50 million (€ 5.36 million). This decision may represent an interesting precedent for other Member States that have strong national air carriers.

10.3. MERGERS AND ACQUISITIONS

Svenska Girot/Bankgirocentralen BGC/Privatgirot/Postgirot

In September 2000, Svenska Girot AB notified its proposed acquisition of sole control over Bankgirocentralen BGC AB (Bankgirot), Privatgirot AB and Postgirot Bank AB. Svenska Girot was owned in equal parts by the four largest banks in

Sweden: Nordbanken AB, Skandinaviska Enskilda Banken AB, Förenings-Sparbanken AB, and Handelsbanken AB, which together account for 80% to 90% of the Swedish banking market. These banks also owned over 90% of the shares in Bankgirot and Privatgirot. Postgirot was a wholly-owned subsidiary of Posten AB, the Swedish postal company.

The target companies all provide services relating to processing and clearing transfers and payment orders between bank accounts. Svenska Girot's stated aim in making the three acquisitions was to achieve economies of scale in processing, netting and clearing payment orders.

On October 30, 2000, the Competition Authority opened an in-depth investigation into the transactions. On February 13, the Authority cleared the acquisitions of Bankgirot and Privatgirot. However, despite far-reaching undertakings offered by Svenska Girot and the four banks, the Competition Authority simultaneously applied to the Stockholm District Court to prohibit Svenska Girot's acquisition of Postgirot. The Competition Authority concluded that the acquisition of Postgirot in combination with the acquisitions of Bankgirot and Privatgirot would give Svenska Girot dominant positions in the markets for distance-payment systems and distance-payment order processing in Sweden. In particular, it found that the proposed concentration would create risks of anti-competitive pricing measures, decreases in innovation, refusals to supply, and other limitations of competition in these markets and a reduction in competition in other banking markets.

In the face of this opposition, Posten terminated the share purchase agreement with Svenska Girot, thereby preventing the case from reaching the Stockholm District Court.

10.4. POLICY AND PROCEDURE

Group Exemption Regulations

The government issued two group exemption regulations regarding certain categories of horizontal cooperation agreements: one concerning R&D agreements, and one concerning specialization agreements. The regulations entered into force on July 1, 2001, and will expire on December 31, 2010. They have the effect of bringing Swedish regulations into line with the Commission's group exemption regulations on R&D and specialization.

11. SWITZERLAND

This section reviews developments concerning the Federal Act of October 6, 1995 on Cartels and Other Restraints of Competition, which is enforced by the Federal Competition Commission (FCC). Appeals against decisions of the FCC are heard by the Appeals Commission for Competition Matters.

11.1. HORIZONTAL AGREEMENTS

Swiss Association of Booksellers/Börsenverein des Deutschen Buchhandels

The Swiss Association of Booksellers and Publishers and the Börsenverein des Deutschen Buchhandels appealed to the Swiss Supreme Court a decision of the Appeals Commission for Competition Matters affirming the FCC's prohibition of a retail price maintenance system in the German-language book industry in Switzerland. The Supreme Court ruled that enforcement of the decision should be suspended until it decides on the merits of the appeal. The Supreme Court noted that the outcome of the case was uncertain and that the immediate enforcement of the decision would lead to quasi-irreversible disruptions.

Betosan/Isotech/Renersco/Weiss et Appetito

On December 17, the FCC charged four undertakings in Bern (Betosan SA, Isotech SA, Renersco SA, and Weiss et Appetito SA) with price-fixing in connection with a tender relating to the restoration of the national library. This is the first FCC decision against a tender (bid-rigging) cartel. The FCC prohibited the four companies from entering into similar concerted practices in future tenders. Fines could be imposed if the undertakings concerned were to breach this prohibition in the future, but the firms were not fined for this violation.

11.2. ABUSE OF MARKET POWER

Teleclub

The Swiss Federal Council dismissed Teleclub SA's appeal against a decision of the Federal Department of Environment, Transport, Energy and Communications that required Teleclub to replace its proprietary "d-box" satellite programming decoder with a "set-top box" equipped with a common interface accessible to other satellite broadcasters. Teleclub, 40% owned by the Kirch Group, is a broadcasting company operating a German-language pay-TV service in Switzerland, and is the dominant provider on that market. The rights to the d-box encryption code are owned by BetaResearch, a Kirch subsidiary.

The regulator's concern is that the d-box, which Teleclub would offer to its subscribers free of charge, is a closed interface that permits the reception solely of programs encrypted with codes controlled by the Kirch group. The Federal Council considered it unlikely that Teleclub's subscribers who already use d-boxes would acquire a second set-top box to receive programs from other broadcasters. Thus, in order to offer their programming to Teleclub d-box subscribers, competing broadcasters would have needed to enter into a license agreement with BetaResearch. The regulators were concerned that BetaResearch would use its position to disadvantage Teleclub's competitors on the pay-TV market and that, due to its affiliation with Teleclub, it would have an interest to do so.

This decision is in conformity with the EU Commission's decisions in the *Bertelsmann/Kirch/Premiere* and *Deutsche Telekom/BetaResearch* cases, as well as with the EU Parliament's draft directive on the legal protection of media diversity in the field of numeric television, which would oblige broadcasters to use common decoder interfaces.

Swisscom

In a dispute between Swisscom and diAx, the Federal Communications Commission ordered Swisscom to partially open the "last mile" of its telecommunications network to diAx pending its final ruling on the merits. However, on Swisscom's application for review, the Swiss Supreme Court held in March that this preliminary order could unnecessarily disadvantage Swisscom and vacated the order.

11.3. MERGERS AND ACQUISITIONS

Banque Nationale de Paris/Paribas

The FCC imposed a fine on Banque Nationale de Paris for failure to notify its acquisition of Paribas to the FCC. The FCC stated that the amount of a fine depends on the market power of the undertakings concerned (determined according to their annual turnover in Switzerland), the degree of restriction on competition, and the risk of elimination of competition. The amount of the fine in this case was not published.

Le Monde/Le Temps

On October 1, the FCC cleared the acquisition by Le Monde of 20.24% of the share capital of Le Temps SA. In this decision, the FCC confirmed that a transaction representing a shift from joint control of an entity by two companies to joint control by three companies may constitute a concentration within the meaning of the Competition Act.

11.4. POLICY AND PROCEDURE

FCC Annual Report

On February 16, the FCC published its annual report for the year 2000. During the year FCC focused on combating hard-core cartels rooted in price-fixing, geographical market sharing and quantity restriction agreements, as well as on acting to repress abuses of dominant positions. Seven investigations were opened and six closed concerning price-fixing agreements, and five were opened and three closed concerning abuses of dominant positions. Charged with analyzing regulations implementing competition policy, the FCC and its Secretariat also devoted attention throughout the year to the electricity and health care markets.

Proposed Amendments to Competition Act

The Swiss Federal Council wishes to toughen the Competition Act by allowing the FCC to impose direct administrative fines on parties to hard-core cartels. A fine of up to 10% of a company's last three annual turnovers is proposed. Also foreseen is a so-called "bonus" system that would mitigate sanctions for firms that voluntarily renounce cartel behavior and/or collaborate with the FCC in exposing cartels.

Introduction of these sanctions, the constitutionality of which has been questioned, has been opposed by management and labor groups and in some political circles.

Foreign Concentrations

The Swiss Supreme Court confirmed that a concentration must be notified in Switzerland as soon as the thresholds provided for in the Competition Act are reached, irrespective of whether the undertakings concerned have a presence in Switzerland. The Court held that if the thresholds are reached, a concentration must presumptively be deemed to have the potential of producing effects on the Swiss market. The concentration must therefore be notified and may not be implemented prior to authorization. Noting that EU merger control also requires prior notification to the European Commission, the Court suggested that notification of a concentration requiring Swiss as well as EU clearance might be simplified for foreign companies by allowing them to file simultaneous notifications to the Commission and to the FCC on forms providing similar data.

Draft Act on Radio and Television

Interested parties had until the end of April to submit their comments on the proposed draft Act on radio and television. Under the draft, the Swiss Broadcasting Corporation (SRG) would receive all radio and television broadcast license fees (which are now split between SRG and private broadcasting companies), but would have to forego advertising revenues. Access to the market would thereby be facilitated for private broadcasting companies in that, among other things, they would no longer be required to have a license.

Most reactions to the proposed draft were unenthusiastic. In particular, SRG noted that the draft law imposes additional restrictions and strengthens government powers. Further, private broadcasting companies requested the ability to retain at least 10% of the license fees and opposed the draft's proposed sponsoring and advertising bans, calling instead for advertising regulations modeled on those in force in other countries.

Life Insurance Market Recommendation

In the context of bilateral negotiations between Switzerland and the EU, on October 1, the FCC issued a recommendation to the Federal Council intended to open the Swiss life insurance market to foreign competition. Under the present legislation, European life insurance companies cannot operate on the Swiss market under the same conditions as Swiss companies. The FCC considers that competition from foreign life insurance companies would exert a positive pressure on the price, quality, and diversity of life insurance offerings in Switzerland.

12. THE UNITED KINGDOM

This section reviews developments concerning the Fair Trading Act of 1973, the Competition Act of 1980, and the Competition Act of 1998, which are enforced by the Competition Commission (CC), the Department of Trade and Industry, the Director General of Fair Trading (DGFT), and the Office of Fair Trading (OFT).

12.1. VERTICAL RESTRAINTS

Termination of Medications Retail Price Maintenance Exemption

The Restrictive Practices Court made an order ending the exemption established in 1970 that allowed resale price maintenance of branded, over-the-counter medications and related goods. The order was imposed after the respondent trade associations withdrew their opposition to the OFT's court action, which followed a preliminary statement by the presiding judge, Justice Buckley, that it was difficult to see how the respondents could argue that the retention of the 1970 exemption was in the public interest. The OFT contends that removing resale price maintenance will lead to lower prices for consumers on a large range of branded medications because of: (i) competition between retail outlets; (ii) pressure from retailers for better terms of supply; and (iii) more competition between rival manufacturers. A further expected benefit will be better service to the public as traditional pharmacists compete with supermarkets by focusing on their own particular strengths.

The OFT had initiated a review of the medications market in 1995 which concluded that resale price maintenance was no longer appropriate and recommended an application to the Court to discharge the 1970 order. In a 1999 hearing, the Court granted the OFT leave to pursue its case after finding that the OFT had presented *prima facie* evidence of a material change in the medications market since the 1970 order was imposed. Over-the-counter medications were the last goods in the United Kingdom on which manufacturers and suppliers could legally set minimum resale prices to the public. In 1997, the Court had struck down a similar exemption relating to books.

12.2. ABUSE OF MARKET POWER

Napp Pharmaceuticals

The OFT imposed its first financial penalty under U.K. competition law in fining Napp Pharmaceuticals, a Cambridge-based pharmaceutical company, £ 3.21 million (€ 5.28 million and about six percent of Napp's sales) for infringing Chapter II of the Competition Act 1998 by abusing its dominant position in the market for the supply of sustained relief morphine (trade name "MST") tablets and capsules in the United Kingdom.[117] Napp was found to have supplied MST to patients in the community at excessively high prices while supplying hospitals at discount levels that blocked competitors.

The OFT concluded that Napp offered discounts of over 90% in tendering for hospital contracts, forcing at least one competitor to withdraw from the market. By retaining its high share of the hospital segment, Napp was able to retain a similarly high share of the much larger business of supplying MST to patients in the community because general practitioner prescriptions are strongly influenced by the brands used in hospitals. Community prices were found to be excessive, typically more than 10 times higher than Napp's hospital prices and six times its export prices.

Reacting to these findings, pharmaceutical industry commentators claimed that offering discounts to bulk buyers was "established practice" in the industry. The OFT has called for evidence that other companies in the industry were engaging in similar discounting policies and for further information from Napp before it decides on any additional measures to regulate Napp's conduct. In particular, the OFT is consulting on whether to impose an obligation on Napp to reduce the price of MST tablets to the community and limit the amount by which community prices can exceed hospital prices.

Banking Sector Complex Monopoly

On March 6, the CC issued its provisional conclusions in its investigation into the supply of banking services by clearing banks to small- and medium-sized enterprises (SMEs). It concluded that a complex monopoly existed among the four

---

[117] This decision was ultimately upheld by the Competition Commission Appeal Tribunal on January 15, 2002, though with a reduction in the amount of the fine to £ 2.2 million.

largest clearing groups (HSBC, Lloyds TSB, Barclays and Royal Bank of Scotland Group) and that they had applied a number of business practices that restricted price competition, resulting in excessive prices and profits.[118]

The investigation concerned a number of markets: (i) liquidity management services, which include business current accounts, overdraft facilities and short-term bank deposit accounts; (ii) general purpose business loans to SMEs; (iii) other types of business loans (such as asset finance) to SMEs; and (iii) other business deposits held by SMEs. Three separate geographical markets (England and Wales, Scotland, and Northern Ireland) were determined to exist for liquidity management services and general purpose business loans, but the other markets for banking services were found to be U.K.-wide. The investigation showed that there was significant market concentration particularly in the markets for liquidity management services, at least 90 per cent of such services in each geographical market being supplied by the four clearing groups. That degree of concentration had changed little over the preceding ten years.

According to the CC's provisional findings, the complex monopoly situation resulted in a situation where the four clearing groups were able to (i) restrict price competition for money transmission charges; (ii) not pay interest on business current accounts; (iii) pay low rates of interest on short-term deposit accounts; (iv) bundle charges for access to relationship managers with other charges; (v) negotiate reduced charges for customers considering switching; (vi) require or encourage SMEs to have business accounts; and (vii) charge for clearing services provided under agency agreements at differential rates not sufficiently related to cost.

The investigation did not reach any conclusions in 2001 as to whether any matter operates or may be expected to operate against the public interest.

---

[118] The investigation was concluded on March 14, 2002, confirming in large part the provisional conclusions. In addition, the final report concluded that certain practices of the clearing groups were against the public interest, in that they resulted in barriers to entry and excessive pricing. Behavioral remedies, including measures to ensure fast error-free switching; the imposition of minimum interest rate on current accounts and/or the elimination of money transmission charge; and price transparency obligations, were recommended and accepted by the DGFT in June 2002.

Yellow Pages

Following the advice of the DGFT, the Secretary of State for Trade and Industry accepted revised undertakings from British Telecommunications Plc (BT) on behalf of Yellow Pages. The revised undertakings include a price cap of RPI minus six on advertising rates effective from January 1, 2002. The DGFT had advised that a tighter price cap than the original RPI minus two, imposed following the 1996 Monopolies and Mergers Commission report on the supply of classified directory advertising services, was needed to protect advertisers from excessive prices, given that Yellow Pages remains dominant in that market. Other parts of the original undertakings were relaxed or removed to provide Yellow Pages with some additional commercial freedom and to reduce the monitoring burden. Yellow Pages will be allowed to publish local directories from May 2003 in addition to its normal regional directories. Yellow Pages is also allowed to deliver directories for neighboring areas in directory border zones without having to make an additional request, provided that it does not charge advertisers more in these circumstances. Yellow Pages was also released from undertakings requiring it to obtain the consent of the DGFT for rate card changes on advertising charges, withdrawal of discount schemes, and changes in the range of advertisement sizes or features or the ordering of entries.

These new undertakings will be reviewed by the DGFT in 2005. The 1996 Monopolies and Mergers Commission report had made adverse findings about the higher prices charged to advertisers by Yellow Pages and about Yellow Pages's publication of local directories, in addition to its normal regional directories, which the Monopolies and Mergers Commission was concerned could weaken competition.

British Sky Broadcasting Limited

The DGFT withdrew undertakings imposed in 1996 on British Sky Broadcasting Limited requiring that it place its basic channel Sky One on its rate card and maintain and provide separate accounts to the OFT. British Sky also accepted new undertakings in relation to its proposed acquisition of control of British Interactive Broadcasting Holdings Limited. The new undertakings require British Sky to provide "clean feed" of premium television channels (*i.e.*, a version of the channel which lacks the interactive elements) to rival distributors. The OFT's December 2000 investigation of British Sky under the Competition Act 1998 is currently expected to be completed by the end of 2002.

Part II: National Competition Developments

Dixons

Dixons was cleared by the OFT of allegations of infringements under the Competition Act 1998. The OFT concluded that Dixons had not infringed competition law by concluding exclusive distribution agreements with Compaq and Packard Bell regarding certain personal computer products. Dixons's share of the market for the supply of home PCs was found to be "considerably below the 40% threshold [the OFT] would normally regard as an indicator of dominance." The OFT confirmed its presumption that Dixons was not dominant by finding a lack of concentration in the home PC market, low barriers to entry, the ease of consumer access to a wide range of PC brands through a variety of outlets, and the lack of strong consumer preferences for one particular PC brand or for purchasing PCs through one particular type of outlet. The OFT also concluded that there were insufficient grounds in this case to exercise the "clawback" power to withdraw the Competition Act's vertical agreement exclusion from the Chapter I prohibition on anti-competitive agreements.

Consignia

Consignia, the new company that has taken over the assets and business of the Post Office, was found not to have breached competition law through its agreement to allow Postal Preference Service Limited (PPS) to use Royal Mail trademarks on consumer lifestyle survey questionnaires. The OFT dismissed allegations from competitors that PPS's use of Royal Mail trademarks was an abuse of a dominant position in breach of Chapter II of the Competition Act in that it would undermine competition in the market for consumer lifestyle data. The OFT based its findings on the fact that: (i) PPS, a joint venture company in which Consignia holds a 44.6% share, had not achieved substantially higher response rates than its competitors; (ii) the Royal Mail trademarks had not markedly improved response rates; and (iii) potential purchasers of PPS data were likely to continue to purchase data from their current suppliers.

General Insurance Standards Council

The Competition Commission Appeal Tribunal rendered its first-ever decision on September 17. The case involved appeals brought by the Institute of Independent Insurance Brokers (IIB) and the Association of British Travel Agents Limited (ABTA) against a decision by the DGFT that a rule imposed by the General Insurance Standards Council (GISC) requiring members to deal only with intermediaries that were also members of GISC did not fall within the Chapter I prohibition.

U.K. insurers formed GISC as a self-regulatory body for the U.K. insurance industry. GISC's rules were binding on its members and, in order to ensure that all independent intermediaries or "brokers" became members of GISC, Rule F42 prohibited members from dealing with any non-member intermediary. However, around 10,000 brokers (over 50% of U.K. brokers), including the members of IIB and ABTA, refused to join GISC. GISC's rules were notified to the DGFT on June 30, 2000, and, despite complaints from IIB and ABTA, the DGFT found on January 24, 2001, that the GISC rules did not fall within the Chapter I prohibition. Following an unsuccessful application to the DGFT for withdrawal or modification of his decision, IIB and ABTA appealed to the Tribunal.

The Tribunal reversed the DGFT's decision, finding that the GISC rules infringed the Chapter I prohibition, and remitted the case to the DGFT for consideration of whether to issue an exemption under Section 4 of the Act. The Tribunal held, first, the GISC rules constituted either an agreement among GISC's members or a decision by an association of undertakings to collectively boycott intermediaries that refused to join GISC. The result would be that intermediaries would have no choice but to join GISC. Second, the limit on the freedom of intermediaries to join self-regulatory bodies was found to be a distortion of competition. Third, because the members of GISC accounted for approximately 85% of insurers active in the United Kingdom, the effect of such distortion would be appreciable. The Tribunal also directed the DGFT to investigate whether the rules would lead to distortion or restriction of competition on the separate market for regulation of insurance intermediaries. There is, as yet, no indication that such investigation has been concluded.

Aberdeen Journals

On July 16, the DGFT fined Aberdeen Journals £ 1.328 million (€ 2.16 million) for predatory conduct on the market for advertising space in local newspapers in the Aberdeen area.[119] Aberdeen Journals had deliberately incurred losses on one of its titles, the *Herald & Post*, in an attempt to expel its only rival, the *Aberdeen & District Independent*. The investigation was opened in January 2000 under the

---

[119] This decision was ultimately set aside by the Competition Commission Appeal Tribunal on March 19, 2002, and remanded to the OFT for reconsideration.

Fair Trading Act, and continued under the Competition Act 1998 following its entry into force on March 1, 2000.

Aberdeen Journals, a member of the Daily Mail group, published two paid-for daily newspapers and one free weekly newspaper, the *Herald & Post*. As a free newspaper, the *Herald & Post* was principally funded by revenues from advertising. The *Aberdeen & District Independent* complained that when it entered the market in 1996, Aberdeen Journals sought to drive it out of the market by reducing advertising rates in the *Herald & Post*, as well as increasing its number of pages and circulation.

The OFT found Aberdeen Journals dominant since it had a 70% share of advertising revenues spent in the relevant market, faced no effective competition (since its only competitor, the *Aberdeen & District Independent*, was subject to an aggressive campaign of predation), and there were barriers to entry (based in part on Aberdeen Journals's reputation for predatory behavior). The OFT further found that the *Herald & Post* sold advertising space at below average total cost until July 2000 and had priced below average variable costs in March, May, and June 2000.

The OFT relied on extensive documentary evidence of Aberdeen Journals's intent to expel the *Aberdeen & District Independent* (including an instruction from Aberdeen Journals's parent company to "keep your foot on their neck!"). While accepting that actions prior to the coming into force of the Act on March 1, 2000, could not themselves be dealt with under the Act, the OFT relied on evidence of such prior actions to prove Aberdeen Journals's continuing intention to act in a predatory manner during March-June 2000.

The OFT concluded that Aberdeen Journals had priced below average variable cost between March 1 and March 29, 2000, raising a presumption of predation that Aberdeen Journals had failed to rebut by providing an objective justification. The predation had adverse effects on the *Aberdeen & District Independent* and raised barriers to entry, and was thus likely to appreciably affect trade within the United Kingdom. In calculating the fine, the OFT took as a starting point 10% (the maximum percentage allowable) of Aberdeen Journals's annual turnover on the relevant market. This amount was then multiplied by a factor of four (to ensure its deterrent effect) and reduced by 30% in recognition of Aberdeen Journals's full cooperation (10%) and cessation of the infringement (20%).

ICL

This investigation had been closed but was re-opened by the DGFT after Synstar, whose earlier complaint had been dismissed, brought a claim in the High Court stating that ICL was abusing a dominant position by not providing certain diagnostic services to customers that obtained hardware maintenance services from companies other than ICL. Synstar argued that this effectively prevented third parties (such as Synstar) from competing for hardware maintenance contracts for ICL mainframes. The Court action was stayed pending the result of the DGFT's investigation.

The DGFT found that ICL was not dominant in the supply of mainframe computers (since it accounted for less than 10% of U.K. hardware sales) or in hardware and software maintenance services (where it accounted for less than 20% of U.K. sales). Moreover, there was no separate "secondary" market for hardware and software maintenance services for ICL computers, since: (1) there was evidence of "whole-life costing" by sophisticated buyers (maintenance was expensive relative to the price of the hardware and the price of maintenance was fully transparent due to tendering procedures); (2) customers were willing to switch away from ICL hardware in response to price increases; and (3) ICL needed to protect its reputation in the highly competitive computer market. Because ICL was not dominant on the "primary market," in the DGFT's view, it could not be dominant on a single market for the primary and secondary products.

Mobile Phone Sector Inquiry

On December 12, the U.K. Office of Telecommunications (Oftel) announced that it would be referring to the Competition Commission its proposal to remedy the excessive mobile phone charges currently imposed on the U.K. market. In its September review of competition for calls to mobile phones, Oftel concluded that mobile termination rates were substantially in excess of cost and that there was little incentive on operators to reduce those charges. Accordingly, Oftel proposes to set a four-year cap of 12% over the retail price index on the BT Cellnet, One2One, Orange, and Vodafone networks. Oftel will, however, conduct a review after two years to determine whether the regulation is still appropriate.

In its review of calls to mobile phones, Oftel concluded that competitive pressures did not exert sufficient constraints on termination charges. Because the caller pays the price of calling a mobile phone and has no choice about the network over which a call is made, there is no incentive on operators to reduce termination charges. Oftel found that, over the last three years, while operators' costs have continued to fall and call volumes have increased, termination charges remained well-above costs. Currently, a peak-rate national call over BT's network is 24 pence for three minutes, while the same call to a mobile network is 60 pence per three minutes, of which 39 pence is the termination charge. Mobile operators argued that mobile termination charges should be considered as part of a whole mobile package, and that higher termination charges were offset by lower prices of calls from mobiles – leading, overall, to revenue growth with no excess profits. Nevertheless, Oftel considered that the termination charges were significantly in excess of costs, and did not represent a fair distribution of costs and benefits between the caller and the owner of the mobile phone. Oftel also found that the broad mobile phone sector was not yet competitive enough to assume that higher profits on incoming calls were balanced out by lower retail prices of outgoing mobile calls. Oftel excluded from its review calls that were carried over third generation (3G) infrastructure.

Three of the mobile operators publicly objected to the proposed charge control. The Director General of Telecommunications has, therefore, referred the matter to the Competition Commission for a decision on whether regulatory actions such as charge controls are in the public interest. The Competition Commission has six months to reach a decision (this period can also be extended for a further six months).

12.3. MERGERS AND ACQUISITIONS

Interbrew

In a landmark ruling, on May 23, the High Court quashed the U.K. competition authorities' decision ordering Interbrew SA to divest Bass Brewers to a single buyer approved by the Director General of Fair Trading (DGFT) on the grounds of procedural unfairness. This is the first successful judicial appeal of a U.K. competition authority decision.

The ruling concerned a merger decision on a completed transaction involving the acquisition by Interbrew of the U.K. brewing interests of Bass plc, namely Bass Holdings Limited (BHL). Interbrew also acquired certain Bass interests outside the United Kingdom, but those aspects of the merger, together with the supply of flavored alcoholic beverages in the United Kingdom, had already been dealt with by the European Commission. The acquisition, which brought together two of the four major national beer brewers and distributors in the United Kingdom, had been referred to the U.K. competition authorities by the European Commission pursuant to Article 9(3)(b) of the Merger Regulation in July 2000 following a request by the U.K. government. The Secretary of State accepted the conclusions of the CC and the advice of the DGFT, Professor John Vickers, and determined that the merger may be expected to operate against the public interest. The Secretary of State therefore concluded that the only adequate remedy would be for Interbrew to divest Bass Brewers in the United Kingdom to a buyer approved by the DGFT.

In defining the relevant market, the CC stated that it was not necessary to decide whether it should be segmented by type of beer since market shares were generally similar under a narrow or broad market definition. Great Britain and Northern Ireland were found to be separate geographic markets. The CC report found that the merger would: (i) make Interbrew (which had acquired the brewing interests of Whitbread plc in 2000) the largest brewer, wholesaler, and distributor of beer in Great Britain; (ii) strengthen Interbrew's portfolio of leading brands, giving it four of the top 10 selling beer brands, including two of the top three (Carling and Stella Artois); and (iii) create an effective duopoly between the two largest brewers/distributors, Interbrew and Scottish & Newcastle. This duopoly was likely to lead to an increase in net wholesale prices. The expected greater emphasis on the promotion of leading brands was also likely to raise barriers to entry and expansion and lead to brand rationalization and, therefore, less consumer choice. The CC also expected that the merger would enhance Interbrew's ability to price-discriminate according to the type of customer, and not simply because of cost differences, making independent wholesalers even less competitive with multiple retailers.

In the High Court, although Justice Moses rejected Interbrew's assertions that the divestment of Bass Brewers was a disproportionate remedy and that the authorities should not have required the sale of Bass Brewers to a single buyer, he held that the CC should have considered evidence from Interbrew that the sale of Whitbread Brewing Company would have been a suitable alternative remedy. In particular, the Court found that Interbrew should have been given the opportunity to comment on whether its "dual capacity" as owner of Bass Brewers and licensor of Stella Artois to Whitbread would have inhibited competition were it to divest Whitbread.

The High Court ordered the Secretary of State for Trade and Industry to reconsider his decision on remedies, with assistance as required from the DGFT. Interested third parties were subsequently asked to comment on potential remedies. The judgment explicitly recognized that the authorities may again reach the same conclusions on remedies "based on the conclusion that Whitbread with Stella Artois would not be a viable and independent force in the market." The judicial review did not challenge the CC's main substantive finding that Interbrew's acquisition of Bass Brewers could be expected to operate against the public interest in that it would strengthen Interbrew's portfolio of leading brands and result in the creation of a duopoly between Interbrew and Scottish & Newcastle.

In the immediate aftermath of the ruling, the CC proclaimed victory on the substance of the case, but CC Chairman Derek Morris later conceded that a review of CC procedures would be required in light of the ruling. The present system (in which potential public interest concerns and hypothetical remedies are discussed concurrently without making clear which competition issues are of concern or how particular remedies may address those concerns) has been criticized for its lack of transparency. Some have called on the CC to adopt a system similar to that of the EU, where competition issues are identified before negotiating remedies with the parties. The Court remitted the question of remedies back to the Secretary of State. Following consultation with the OFT, the Secretary of State then decided that a lesser divestment – involving the Carling brands only – would be sufficient for approval of the acquisition.

Lloyds TSB/Abbey National

On July 10, the Secretary of State for Trade and Industry blocked Lloyds TSB's proposed acquisition of Abbey National after the CC identified adverse effects in respect of the personal current account and SME markets.[120] Lloyds TSB was one of the "Big Four" U.K. banks (Barclays, HSBC, Lloyds TSB and Royal Bank of Scotland/National Westminster Bank) and Abbey National was a comparatively recent entrant into full-service banking, having been formed as a mutual society.

The banks competed in several markets: financial products sold to personal customers, including personal current accounts (PCAs), mortgages and savings accounts; financial products sold to small and medium-sized enterprises (SMEs); financial products sold to larger firms; and wholesale banking. No concerns arose in relation to financial products sold to larger firms or wholesale banking due to the presence of worldwide markets, strong global players and strong buyers. Similarly, the markets for mortgages and savings accounts were competitive. Concerns arose, however, in relation to PCAs and financial products sold to SMEs.

In PCAs, the transaction would have increased Lloyds TSB's already-leading market share from 22% to 27% and would have raised the combined market share of the Big Four from 72% to 77%. Given this market structure, the Competition Commission noted that there were several characteristics of the PCA market, including homogeneous products, a lack of customer buyer power, transparency of prices, stability of demand, and similarity of size and cost structure among suppliers that, when considered together with the Big Four's past conduct, made the

---

[120] Ultimately, on February 18, 2002, the Secretary of State accepted undertakings preventing Lloyds TSB from acquiring Abbey National's personal current account or SME businesses. Accordingly, the undertakings do not prevent Lloyds TSB acquiring any other part of Abbey National's business which might come up for sale.

market vulnerable to tacit collusion in pricing. The Competition Commission also noted significant "constraints on the development of competition" caused by the entrenched position of the Big Four, reluctance of consumers to switch PCAs, limited growth of non-branch-based banks, and the inability of new branch-based banks to grow their market shares. Abbey National, however, was a successful and innovative alternative supplier capable of maintaining its independence or merging with another player to form an enlarged fifth bank.

The Competition Commission similarly found that the market for SME financial products was dominated by the Big Four banks, which had a combined and stable share of around 85% (Lloyds TSB had 16%), and there were high barriers to entry. Again, Abbey National was perceived as a significant competitive threat: although it accounted for less than 1% of the market, it had all the characteristics needed to succeed as a new entrant.

The Competition Commission considered a number of proposed remedies, including divestitures of smaller banks owned by Lloyds TSB or of packages of branches, and behavioral undertakings in relation to services and charges, but concluded that prohibiting the merger was the only remedy capable of addressing the identified concerns.[121]

Govia/Connex

On July 20, under Article 9(2)(b) of the EC Merger Regulation, the European Commission referred to the U.K. competition authorities the proposed transfer of the South Central Rail Franchise from Connex to Govia. The case, which was subsequently approved by the Secretary of State without a reference to the Competition Commission, was the 11th time a referral has been requested by the United Kingdom. Eight of these requests have been granted. (Previous cases referred include *C3D/Rhone Capital/GoAhead* (2000), *Interbrew/Bass* (2000), *Hanson/Pioneer International* (2000), *Anglo American/Tarmac* (1999), *Redland/Lafarge* (1997), *GEHE/Lloyds* (1996) and *Tarmac/Steetley* (1992).)

---

[121] Interestingly, on July 19, the Secretary of State for Trade and Industry approved the merger between Halifax plc and Bank of Scotland, noting that "this merger does not involve one of the Big Four banks and the removal of a competitor. In fact, it may strengthen competitive pressures on the Big Four."

Part II: National Competition Developments

Promatech/Sulzer

In December, the Secretary of State, together with the Italian, German and Spanish competition authorities jointly referred to the European Commission the Italian company Promatech S.p.A.'s proposed acquisition of the Swiss firm Sulzer AG's weaving machines business (see above under Germany, Italy and Spain). This was the first time the United Kingdom requested a referral under Article 22.

Cargill/Cerestar

On December 20, the European Commission granted the U.K. Government's request, under Article 9(2)(a) of the EC Merger Regulation, to refer review of the proposed acquisition by Cargill, Incorporated of Cerestar International to the U.K. authorities.

12.4. POLICY AND PROCEDURE

Transport Ticket Block Exemption

The government, on the advice of the DGFT, decided that ticketing schemes for local travel on buses, trains, trams and inland ferries (*i.e.*, multi-operator travelcards, multi-operator individual tickets, through tickets and add-ons) can be made the subject of a block exemption from Chapter I of the Competition Act 1998. The OFT is preparing industry guidelines to explain what type of schemes this block exemption will cover and how it will work. The DGFT warned that the block exemption will not allow public transport operators to get together to fix ordinary single and return fares or share routes.

Competition Regime Reforms

As part of the government's "Enterprise for All" initiative, the Secretary of State for Trade and Industry, Patricia Hewitt, announced that a White Paper would be published in July setting out proposals to reform the U.K. competition regime.[122]

---

[122] These proposals have been incorporated in the U.K. government's Enterprise Bill, which was presented before Parliament on March 26, 2002.

The proposals include: (i) making U.K. competition authorities fully independent of political influence and promoting transparent procedures and enhanced parliamentary accountability; (ii) giving the OFT and CC a formal role in advising on public sector regulations that could be anti-competitive; and (iii) consulting on introducing a new criminal offense for individuals engaged in cartels, which would be in line with U.S. measures but contrary to practices in the EU and individual Member States. These supplement the planned merger reform proposals. CC procedures on remedies may also be revised in light of the High Court's findings in the Interbrew judicial review.

In the OFT, a new advisory panel was established in May that will meet monthly. The members are Michelle Childs of the Consumers Association; John Mills, a former OFT Director of Consumer Affairs; Sir Geoffrey Owen, fellow at the London School of Economics and a former editor of the *Financial Times*; and Richard Whish, Professor of Law at King's College, London. The panel will advise on the OFT's strategy, new policy developments, areas for research and debate, market analysis, and communications. The panel will not have executive powers and is strictly advisory. According to the OFT, this panel is not meant as a precursor to the statutory board proposed by the government in its September 2000 consultation paper on the "Proposed New Structure for the OFT."

Proposed Criminalization of "Hard Core" Cartel Activities

On November 28, the OFT published an independent report on how a proposed new regime of criminal sanctions for cartel perpetrators could best operate in practice. The report proposes the criminalization of four types of "hard core" cartel activities: price-fixing, market-sharing, bid-rigging, and agreeing to restrict output or set quotas. The OFT's main recommendations include: (a) that the criminal offence be built on the concept of individuals dishonestly entering into cartel arrangements with each other; (b) that the Serious Fraud Office be the lead prosecutor, working closely with the OFT; (c) that companies and other undertakings continue to be subject to the existing civil sanctions; (d) that the maximum penalty for individuals found guilty of having committed criminal antitrust offences be at least a custodial sentence of 5 years imprisonment; and (e) that the courts have the power to impose, without any restriction as to amount, a fine, either in addition to, or instead of, a custodial sentence on conviction.

The criminal offence is intended to apply only to horizontal agreements between individuals representing "competing" undertakings operating at the same level of the supply chain. It is not to apply to vertical agreements, many of which the OFT considers to have pro-competitive or other beneficial effects. These are

Part II: National Competition Developments

also currently excluded from the application of the Chapter I prohibition, and may benefit from exemptions under European competition law. The criminal offence is also intended to cover those who aid, abet, or incite the substantive offence, as well as anyone who continues to participate in a cartel where the initial agreement was entered into before the new criminalization provisions come into force. However the offence is defined, it seems likely that the OFT will publish guidelines detailing the approach to be taken in prosecuting these offences, and stating that the prosecutor will always retain discretion not to prosecute a case.

The Government's proposal to criminalize "hard core" cartel activities will bring with it a requirement that investigators comply with all legislative procedures presently required under the U.K. criminal justice system (most importantly, that the standard of proof justifying an investigation be the higher, criminal standard of guilt beyond reasonable doubt). By contrast, the Competition Act 1998 currently gives the Director General of the Office of Fair Trading civil powers of investigation to determine whether there has been an infringement of the Chapter I prohibition based on a "balance of probability" standard.

Given the significance of covertly-obtained evidence of cartel behavior, the report recommends that OFT investigators be authorized to carry out intrusive surveillance, property interference, and interception of communications (within the rules of the existing criminal justice system). The report also recommends that all investigations that are likely to proceed toward a possible criminal prosecution be conducted accordingly to criminal prosecutorial standards (including rules of evidence and procedure) from the outset. It further recommends that, wherever possible, criminal proceedings against individuals precede any related civil proceedings against undertakings in an effort to preclude arguments by criminal defendants that their case had been prejudiced.

Although the report offers a comprehensive policy on the criminalization of "hard core" cartel activity, it notably omits any discussion of the treatment of individuals who inform on other cartel participants. The OFT makes no specific policy recommendation on leniency for whistle-blowers, but merely states that such a policy ought to be consistent with the existing leniency policies operated under civil procedures in both the United Kingdom and before the European Commission with respect to undertakings.

Competition in Professions Report

The DGFT, in publishing his report on "Competition in Professions" on March 7 (which addresses the legal, accountancy and architectural professions), stated that the professions should be fully subject to competition law and unjustified restrictions on competition should be removed. The DGFT's report was prepared following a review by the Law and Economics Consulting Group commissioned by his predecessor. The Secretary of State for Trade and Industry supported the DGFT's recommendation to remove the exclusion for professional rules from the Competition Act 1998's Chapter I prohibition on anti-competitive agreements and noted that consultations will take place on the restrictions identified by the DGFT.[123]

Other restrictions that the DGFT's report noted as needing to be addressed include: (i) operation of the Queen's Counsel system for barristers as a "quality mark" and its value to consumers; (ii) professional rules that prevent or hinder multi-disciplinary practices; (iii) anti-competitive restrictions on access to lawyers (*e.g.*, requirements that solicitors employed by non-solicitors act only for their employers, that barristers not have direct access to clients, and that independent barristers not conduct litigation); (iv) the bar against solicitors and accountants making payments to third parties for work referred to them, potentially hampering the development of on-line marketplaces that could bring clients and professionals together; (v) the Law Society prohibition on seeking business by "cold calls" to potential clients and comparative fee advertising; (vi) non-implementation of the Courts and Legal Services Act that, if implemented, would enable banks and building societies to provide conveyancing services and increase competition for probate services; (vii) the perception of professional legal privilege as a means of distorting competition in favor of lawyers; (viii) non-binding fee guidance issued by the Royal Institute of British Architects and the Law Society that could restrict or distort price competition; and (ix) the "50% rule" that restricts statutory audits to those who practice in a firm in which qualified accountants hold the majority of voting rights.

---

[123] A progress report was published by the DGFT in April 2002. The results were that each of the professional bodies concerned had taken some positive action towards removing unjustified restrictions, and therefore, the investigation would continue.

TABLE OF CASES

AB/Provinzial (Denmark)	93
Aberdeen Journals (United Kingdom)	151
Accor/Sodhexo/Chèque-Déjeuner (France)	101
Adria-Wien Pipeline v Finanzlandesdirektion für Kärnten (EC)	58
ADtranz/Bombardier (EC)	38
Agreement between Nordic Competition Authorities (Denmark)	94
Alitalia (I) (Italy)	118
Alitalia (II) (Italy)	119
Ambulanz Glöckner v Landkreis Südwestpfalz (EC)	12
Amendments to Competition Law (France)	103
Amendments to Competition Law (Italy)	122
Amendments to Competition Law (Spain)	135
Amino Acids (EC)	72
Austria v Commission (EC)	55
Austrian Postal Operator (Austria)	79
Banking Sector Cartel (France)	100
Banking Sector Complex Monopoly (United Kingdom)	147
Banque Nationale de Paris/Paribas (Switzerland)	143
BASF/Eurodiol/Pantochim (EC)	42
Benetton (France)	99
Betosan/Isotech/Renersco/Weiss et Appetito (Switzerland)	141
Boeing/Jeppesen Group (France)	102
BP/Veba Oel; Shell/DEA (Germany)	109
BP Chemicals/Solvay (EC)	54
British Sky Broadcasting Limited (United Kingdom)	149
BVBA Incine/NV Rendac (Belgium)	84
Callahan Associates/NetCologne (Germany)	106
Canal+ (France)	97
Cargill/Cerestar (United Kingdom)	158

Table of Cases

Carlsberg (Denmark)	90
Carlsberg/Coca-Cola Bottlers (Denmark)	94
Cepsa/Repsol (Spain)	129
Change in Competition Authority Status (The Netherlands)	124
Communication on Vertical Agreements (Greece)	112
Competition Authority 2000 Annual Report (The Netherlands)	125
Competition in Professions Report (United Kingdom)	160
Competition Regime Reforms (United Kingdom)	158
Concrete Industry Cartel (France)	101
Consignia (United Kingdom)	150
Construction Industry Cartel (France)	101
Cooperative and Concentrative Joint Ventures (Austria)	82
Corus UK Ltd. v Commission (EC)	69
Council Annual Report (Belgium)	87
Courage v Crehan (EC)	3
Covisint (EC)	52
Dairy Cartel (Spain)	128
Danish Football Association (Denmark)	90
Dansk Kørelærer Union (Denmark)	91
De Beers/Rio Tinto/Ashton Mining; P&O/Antwerp Combined Terminals (Belgium)	85
De Minimis Notice (EC)	75
Decree on Merger Control Procedure (Spain)	135
Degussa/Laporte (EC)	46
Den Almindelige Danske Lægeforening (Denmark)	89
Deutsche Lufthansa/Eurowings (Germany)	107
Deutsche Post (EC)	16
Deutsche Post (EC)	21
Deutsche Post/trans-o-flex Schnell-Lieferdienst (Germany)	108
Dixons (United Kingdom)	150
DONG/Naturgas Sjælland (Denmark)	92
Draft Act on Radio and Television (Switzerland)	144

Table of Cases

Draft Guidelines on Market Analysis and the Calculation of Significant Market Power for Electronic Communications Networks and Services (EC)	23
Draft Law regarding Regional Competition Authorities (Spain)	134
Draft Leniency Notice (EC)	73
Draft Regulation on Agreements Qualifying for EC Block Exemptions (Spain)	133
Duales System Deutschland AG (EC)	18
EDF/EnBW (EC)	36
Electricity Sector Decision Body (Germany)	110
Electricity Sector Proceedings (Germany)	105
Empresa Mixta de Servicios Funerarios de Madrid (Spain)	130
Endesa/Iberdrola (Spain)	130
Enel/France Télécom/Infostrada (Italy)	121
FCC Annual Report (Switzerland)	143
Ferring v Agence Centrale des Organismes de Sécurité Sociale (EC)	60
Fining Guidelines (The Netherlands)	126
Foreign Concentrations (Switzerland)	144
Format/profil (Austria)	80
France Télécom (France)	68
General Application of the Leniency Notice (EC)	75
General Electric/Honeywell (EC)	31
General Insurance Standards Council (United Kingdom)	150
Glaxo Wellcome Dual Pricing System (EC)	5
GlaxoWellcome (Greece)	113
Goodyear/Michelin (Germany)	105
Govia/Connex (United Kingdom)	157
Granarolo/Centrale del Latte di Vicenza (Italy)	120
Group Exemption Regulations (Sweden)	140
Hidroelectrica del Cantabrico/Villar Mir/EnBW (EC)	39
Hitachi/LG Electronics (EC)	53
Højgaard & Schultz/Monberg & Thorsen (Denmark)	94
Hutchinson/NTT DoCoMo/KPN Mobile (EC)	52
Hutchinson/RMPM/ECT (EC)	40

Table of Cases

Iberdrola Redes (Spain)	132
IBM Italia/Business Solutions (EC)	51
ICL (United Kingdom)	152
IMS HEALTH (EC)	20
Inter-bank Charge for Eurocheque Card Payments (Germany)	104
Interbrew (United Kingdom)	154
Intervention of the Competition Council before the Court of Appeals (Belgium)	87
Irish Sugar v Commission (EC)	15
Kirch Group/EM.TV (Germany)	105
Krupp Thyssen Stainless GmbH and Acciai Speciali Terni SpA v Commission (EC)	71
La Casera (Spain)	127
La Poste France (EC)	22
Le Monde/Le Temps (Switzerland)	143
Lekkerland/Tobaccoland (Germany)	106
Life Insurance Market Recommendation (Switzerland)	144
Linde-Verlag/Wolters Kluwer (Austria)	81
Lloyds TSB/Abbey National (United Kingdom)	156
Madrid Airport Cargo Operators (Spain)	127
MAN/Auwärter (EC)	41
Mannesmannröhren-Werke AG v Commission (EC)	65
Métropole Télévision (M6), Suez-Lyonnaise des Eaux, France Télécom and Télévision Française 1 SA (TF1) v Commission (EC)	68
Metsä Tissue/SCA Mölnlycke (EC)	29
Michelin (EC)	6
Mobile Phone Sector Inquiry (United Kingdom)	153
Napp Pharmaceuticals (United Kingdom)	147
Nestlé/Ralston Purina (EC)	47
"New Hearing" Rule in Merger Proceedings (Belgium)	86
New Merger Notification Thresholds (Belgium)	87
New Merger Notification Thresholds (Italy)	123
New Merger Notification Thresholds (The Netherlands)	125
Non-Cash Payment Systems (Austria)	80

Table of Cases

Nordic Competition Meeting (Denmark)	94
Notice on Remedies (EC)	26
Nutreco España/Agrovic Alimentación (Spain)	131
OECD Recommendation on Tribunal (Spain)	134
Opel Danmark (Denmark)	91
Otis/Ceam/Kone/Schindler (Italy)	115
Philips/Marconi Medical Systems (EC)	48
Pio Coronado/Cemetro (Spain)	131
Portugal v Commission (EC)	10
Portuguese Republic v Commission (EC)	58
PreussenElektra v Schlesswag (EC)	56
Promatech/Sulzer (Germany)	109
Promatech/Sulzer (Italy)	122
Promatech/Sulzer (Spain)	132
Promatech/Sulzer (United Kingdom)	158
Proposed Amendments to Competition Act (Denmark)	95
Proposed Amendments to Competition Act (Switzerland)	143
Proposed Criminalization of "Hard Core" Cartel Activities (United Kingdom)	159
Ready-Mixed Concrete Industry Cartel (Germany)	104
Real Estate Franchise Chain (Denmark)	90
Regione Autonoma Friuli-Venezia Giulia v Commission (EC)	63
Removal of Members of the Competition Service (Belgium)	87
RJB Mining v Commission (EC)	62
Ruko (Denmark)	92
Sanacorp/Andreae-Noris Zahn (Germany)	108
Scandinavian Airline System (Sweden)	138
Schneider Electric/Legrand (EC)	33
Seagram/Pernod Ricard/Diageo (EC)	46
Seat Pagine Gialle/Cecchi Gori Communications (Italy)	119
Smith & Nephew/Beiersdorf (EC)	49
Svenska Girot/Bankgirocentralen BGC/Privatgirot/Postgirot (Sweden)	139
Swiss Association of Booksellers/Börsenverein des Deutschen Buchhandels (Switzerland)	141

Table of Cases

Swisscom (Switzerland)	142
Tate & Lyle, British Sugar and Napier Brown v Commission (EC)	66
Teleclub (Switzerland)	142
Telecom Italia (Italy)	117
Telecom Italia Mobile/Omnitel Pronto Italia (Italy)	116
Telefónica Móviles (Spain)	129
Termination of Medications Retail Price Maintenance Exemption (United Kingdom)	146
Terra Networks/Banco Bilbao Vizcaya Argentaria (Spain)	133
Tetra Pak/Sidel (EC)	34
The Post Office/TNT/Singapore Post (EC)	49
TNT Traco v Poste Italiane (EC)	11
T-Online/TUI/C&N (EC)	50
Transport Ticket Block Exemption (United Kingdom)	158
Tryg Baltica (Denmark)	89
Unione Petrolifera (Italy)	116
United Airlines/US Air (EC)	44
UPM-Kymmene/Norske Skog/Haindl (EC)	43
Uponor/Aktiebolaget Svenska Wavin/KWH PIPE Sverige (Sweden)	138
VEBA/VIAG; RWE/VEW (Germany)	107
Vinci/Groupe GTM (Belgium)	85
Yellow Pages (United Kingdom)	149

KEYWORD INDEX

abuse of market position (see blacklisting, cross-subsidization, discriminatory/
differential pricing or conditions, dominant position, excessive pricing, exclusive
rights, fidelity incentives, price undercutting, refusal to supply goods or services,
remedies)

annual reports
   Council Annual Report (Belgium)   87
   Competition Authority 2000 Annual Report (The Netherlands)   125
   FCC Annual Report (Switzerland)   143

barriers to market entry
   Draft Market Analysis Guidelines (EC)   23
   Metsä Tissue/SCA Mölnlycke (EC)   29
   United Airlines/US Air (EC)   44
   Ruko (Denmark)   92
   France Télécom (France)   68
   Granarolo/Centrale del Latte di Vicenza (Italy)   120
   Dixons (United Kingdom)   150
   Aberdeen Journals (United Kingdom)   151

bias
   Removal of Members of the Competition Service (Belgium)   87

blacklisting
   Telefónica Móviles (Spain)   129

block exemptions
   Draft Regulation on Agreements Qualifying for EC Block Exemptions (Spain)   133
   Group Exemption Regulations (Sweden)   140
   Transport Ticket Block Exemption (United Kingdom)   158
   Termination of Medications Retail Price Maintenance Exemption (United Kingdom)   146
   Competition in Professions Report (United Kingdom)   160

bonus scheme (*see* fidelity rebates)

cartels (*see* horizontal agreements)

civil procedure
   applicability in competition proceedings:
   "New Hearing" Rule in Merger Proceedings (Belgium)   86

collective dominance (*see* dominant position)

Keyword Index

commitments (*see* undertakings)

competitive constraints
  Metsä Tissue/SCA Mölnlycke (EC) 29
  Tetra Pak/Sidel (EC) 34
  EDF/EnBW (EC) 36
  UPM-Kymmene/Norske Skog/Haindl (EC) 43
  Philips/Marconi Medical Systems (EC) 48
  Format/profil (Austria) 80
  Alitalia (II) (Italy) 119
  Enel/France Télécom/Infostrada (Italy) 121

complex monopoly
  Banking Sector Complex Monopoly (United Kingdom) 147

concentration, existence of (*see also* full functionality of joint venture; control)
  Hutchinson/RMPM/ECT (EC) 40
  Linde-Verlag/Wolters Kluwer (Austria) 81
  Le Monde/Le Temp (Switzerland) 143

consummation of merger, pre-clearance
  exemption from general prohibition:
  Deutsche Post/trans-o-flex Schnell-Lieferdienst (Germany) 108
  penalties for violating prohibition:
  Competition Authority 2000 Annual Report (The Netherlands) 125
  remedies:
  Schneider Electric/Legrand (EC) 33
  Interbrew (United Kingdom) 154

control
  decisive influence:
  Decree on Merger Control Procedure (Spain) 135
  joint control:
  Covisint (EC) 52
  IBM Italia/Business Solutions (EC) 51
  Hutchinson/NTT DoCoMo/KPN Mobile (EC) 52
  Terra Networks/Banco Bilbao Vizcaya Argentaria (Spain) 133
  Callahan Associates/NetCologne (Germany) 106

cooperation among competition authorities (*see also* referral)
  Agreement between Nordic Competition Authorities (Denmark) 94
  Nordic Competition Meeting (Denmark) 94
  Promatech/Sulzer (Germany, Italy, Spain, United Kingdom) 109, 122, 132, 158

criminal proceedings 160
  Proposed Criminalization of "Hard Core" Cartel Activities (United Kingdom) 159

cross-subsidization
  Deutsche Post (EC) 16
  BVBA Incine/NV Rendac (Belgium) 84

de minimis (*see* jurisdictional thresholds)

discriminatory/differential pricing or conditions
  Glaxo Wellcome Dual Pricing System (EC) 5
  Michelin (EC) 6
  Portugal v Commission (EC) 10
  Deutsche Post (II) (EC) 21
  Metsä Tissue/SCA Mölnlycke (EC) 29
  Ruko (Denmark) 92
  France Télécom (France) 68
  Alitalia (I) (Italy) 118
  Empresa Mixta de Servicios Funerarios de Madrid (Spain) 130
  Teleclub (Switzerland) 142
  Napp Pharmaceuticals (United Kingdom) 147
  Banking Sector Complex Monopoly (United Kingdom) 147

discriminatory taxation
  between Member States:
  Portuguese Republic v Commission (EC) 58
  within a Member State:
  Adria-Wien Pipeline v Finanzlandesdirektion für Kärnten (EC) 58
  Ferring v Agence Centrale des Organismes de Sécurité Sociale (EC) 60

divestitures (*see* undertakings)

dominant position
  and abusive conduct, causal relationship between:
  Austrian Postal Operator (Austria) 79
  collective dominance:
  Draft Market Analysis Guidelines (EC) 23
  MAN/Auwärter (EC) 41
  UPM-Kymmene/Norske Skog/Haindl (EC) 43
  Philips/Marconi Medical Systems (EC) 48
  Granarolo/Centrale del Latte di Vicenza (Italy) 120
  Banking Sector Complex Monopoly (United Kingdom) 147
  Lloyds TSB/Abbey National (United Kingdom) 156
  Interbrew (United Kingdom) 154
  dominant purchaser position:
  Alitalia (I) (Italy) 118
  elimination of competitive constraint:
  Tetra Pak/Sidel (EC) 34

eliminator of competitor:
EDF/EnBW (EC)   36
Philips/Marconi Medical Systems (EC)   48
Deutsche Post/trans-o-flex Schnell-Lieferdienst (Germany)   108
Svenska Girot/Bankgirocentralen BGC/Privatgiro/Postgirot (Sweden)   139
existence, creation or strengthening of, generally:
Draft Market Analysis Guidelines (EC)   23
Hutchinson/RMPM/ECT (EC)   40
T-Online/TUI/C&N (EC)   50
Linde-Verlag/Wolters Kluwer (Austria)   81
AB/Provinzial (Denmark)   93
Deutsche Lufthansa/Eurowings (Germany)   107
Sanacorp/Andrae-Noris Zahn (Germany)   108
Enel/France Télécom/Infostrada (Italy)   121
Banking Sector Complex Monopoly (United Kingdom)   147
Dixons (United Kingdom)   150
ICL (United Kingdom)   152
Højgaard & Schultz/Monberg & Thorsen (Denmark)   94
BVBA Incine/NV Rendac (Belgium)   84
Seat Pagine Gialle/Cecchi Gori Communications (Italy)   119
horizontal overlaps:
General Electric/Honeywell (EC)   31
Schneider Electric/Legrand (EC)   33
Non-Cash Payment Systems (Austria)   80
Svenska Girot/Bankgirocentralen BGC/Privatgiro/Postgirot (Sweden)   139
third party dominant position:
Hidroelectrica del Cantabrico/Villar Mir/EnBW (EC)   39
Callahan Associates/NetCologne (Germany)   106

duopoly (*see* collective dominance)

essential facilities
  Draft Market Analysis Guidelines (EC)   23
  Electricity Sector Decision Body (Germany)   110
  Telecom Italia (Italy)   117

European Convention on Human Rights
  Mannesmannröhren-Werke AG v Commission (EC)   65

evidence
  required to prove cartel:
  Telecom Italia Mobile/Omnitel Pronto Italia (Italy)   116
  Unione Petrolifera (Italy)   116
  Dairy Cartel (Spain)   128

Keyword Index

   required to show excessive pricing:
   Alitalia (II) (Italy)   119
   use of pre-prohibition conduct to show post-prohibition violations:
   Aberdeen Journals (United Kingdom)   151

excessive pricing
   Deutsche Post (EC)   16
   Deutsche Post (II) (EC)   21
   Non-Cash Payment Systems (Austria)   80
   Electricity Sector Proceedings (Germany)   105
   Electricity Sector Decision Body (Germany)   110
   Alitalia (II) (Italy)   119
   Napp Pharmaceuticals (United Kingdom)   147
   Yellow Pages (United Kingdom)   149
   Mobile Phone Sector Inquiry (United Kingdom)   153

exclusive rights
   TNT Traco v Poste Italiene (EC)   11
   Ambulanz Glöckner v Landkreis Südwestpfalz (EC)   12
   La Poste France (EC)   22
   Austrian Postal Operator (Austria)   79
   Seat Pagine Gialle/Cecchi Gori Communications (Italy)   119

exclusivity provisions
   Courage v Crehan (EC)   3
   Tryg Baltica (Denmark)   89
   Den Almindelige Danske Lægeforening (Denmark)   89
   Carlsberg (Denmark)   90
   Danish Football Association (Denmark)   90
   Canal+ (France)   97
   Benetton (France)   99
   La Casera (Spain)   127
   Cepsa/Repsol (Spain)   129
   Dixons (United Kingdom)   150

exercise of offical authority
   Ambulanz Glöckner v Landkreis Südwestpfalz (EC)   12

"failing firm" doctrine
   BASF/Eurodiol/Pantochim (EC)   42
   Format/profil (Austria)   80

failure to notify (*see* notification)

failure to serve decision within prohibition period
   Linde-Verlag/Wolters Kluwer (Austria)   81

173

Keyword Index

fidelity incentives
  Michelin (EC) 6
  Deutsche Post (EC) 16
  Opel Danmark (Denmark) 91
  Alitalia (I) (Italy) 118
  Scandinavian Airline System (Sweden) 138
fines
  adequacy of:
  Competition Authority 2000 Annual Report (The Netherlands) 125
  aggravating factors:
  Michelin (EC) 6
  Banking Sector Cartel (France) 100
  Concrete Industry Cartel (France) 101
  Fining Guidelines (The Netherlands) 126
  Cepsa/Repsol (Spain) 129
  amounts, generally:
  Deutsche Post (EC) 16
  Deutsche Post (II) (EC) 21
  Michelin (EC) 6
  Tate & Lyle, British Sugar and Napier Brown v Commission (EC) 66
  Krupp Thyssen Stainless GmbH and Acciai Speciali Terni SpA v Commission (EC) 71
  Amino Acids (EC) 72
  General Application of the Leniency Notice (EC) 75
  Banking Sector Cartel (France) 100
  Accor/Sodhexo/Chèque Déjeuner (France) 101
  Concrete Industry Cartel (France) 101
  Construction Industry Cartel (France) 101
  France Télécom (France) 68
  Ready-Mixed Concrete Industry Cartel (Germany) 104
  Alitalia (I) (Italy) 118
  Madrid Airport Cargo Operators (Spain) 127
  Telefónica Móviles (Spain) 129
  Cepsa/Repsol (Spain) 129
  Empresa Mixta de Servicios Funerarios de Madrid (Spain) 130
  Uponor/Aktiebolaget Svenska Wavin/KWH PIPE Sverige (Sweden) 138
  Scandinavian Airline System (Sweden) 138
  Napp Pharmaceuticals (United Kingdom) 147
  Aberdeen Journals (United Kingdom) 151
  calculation methodology:
  Deutsche Post (II) (EC) 21
  Michelin (EC) 6
  Krupp Thyssen Stainless GmbH and Acciai Speciali Terni SpA v Commission (EC) 71

Keyword Index

    Proposed Amendments to Competition Act (Denmark) 95
    Concrete Industry Cartel (France) 101
    Amendments to Competition Law (Italy) 122
    Fining Guidelines (The Netherlands) 126
    Proposed Amendments to Competition Act (Switzerland) 143
    Aberdeen Journals (United Kingdom) 151
    equal treatment:
    Krupp Thyssen Stainless GmbH and Acciai Speciali Terni SpA v Commission (EC) 71
    interest on fine refunds:
    Corus UK Ltd. v Commission (EC) 69
    leniency:
    Tate & Lyle, British Sugar and Napier Brown v Commission (EC) 66
    Krupp Thyssen Stainless GmbH and Acciai Speciali Terni SpA v Commission (EC) 71
    Amino Acids (EC) 72
    Draft Leniency Notice (EC) 73
    General Application of the Leniency Notice (EC) 75
    Amendments to Competition Law (France) 103
    Competition Authority 2000 Annual Report (The Netherlands) 125
    Proposed Amendments to Competition Act (Switzerland) 143
    Aberdeen Journals (United Kingdom) 151
    mitigating factors:
    Deutsche Post (EC) 16
    Deutsche Post (II) (EC) 21
    Duales System Deutschland AG (EC) 18
    Aberdeen Journals (United Kingdom) 151

free movement of goods
    GlaxoWellcome Dual Pricing System (EC) 5

full functionality of joint venture
    Hitachi/LG Electronics (EC) 53
    BP Chemicals/Solvay (EC) 54
    Cooperative and Concentrative Joint Ventures (Austria) 82
    Proposed Amendments to Competition Act (Denmark) 95
    Decree on Merger Control Procedure (Spain) 135

government price intervention
    GlaxoWellcome Dual Pricing System (EC) 5

Herfindal-Hirschman Index
    Granarolo/Centrale del Latte di Vicenza (Italy) 120

horizontal agreements
    allocation of markets:
    Banking Sector Cartel (France) 100

Keyword Index

    Construction Industry Cartel (France) 101
    Accor/Sodhexo/Chèque Déjeuner (France) 101
    Uponor/Aktiebolaget Svenska Wavin/KWH PIPE Sverige (Sweden) 138
    "conscious parallelism":
    Dairy Cartel (Spain) 128
    criminalization:
    Proposed Criminalization of "Hard Core" Cartel Activities (United Kingdom) 159
    generally:
    Inter-bank Charge for Eurocheque Payments (Germany) 104
    Otis/Ceam/Kone/Schindler (Italy) 115
    Madrid Airport Cargo Operators (Spain) 127
    Swiss Association of Booksellers/Börsenverein des Deutschen Buchhandels (Switzerland) 141
    General Insurance Standards Council (United Kingdom) 150
    price-fixing:
    Concrete Industry Cartel (France) 101
    Ready-Mixed Concrete Industry Cartel (Germany) 104
    Telecom Italia Mobile/Omnitel Pronto Italia (Italy) 116
    Unione Petrolifera (Italy) 116
    Uponor/Aktiebolaget Svenska Wavin/KWH PIPE Sverige (Sweden) 138
    Betosan/Isotech/Renersco/Weiss et Appetito (Switzerland) 141

intellectual property
    Duales System Deutschland AG (EC) 18
    IMS Health (EC) 20
    Consignia (United Kingdom) 150

interim measures
    Duales System Deutschland AG (EC) 18
    IMS Health (EC) 20
    Removal of Members of the Competition Service (Belgium) 87
    Canal+ (France) 97
    GlaxoWellcome (Greece) 113
    Swiss Association of Booksellers/Börsenverein des Deutschen Buchhandels (Switzerland) 141
    Swisscom (Switzerland) 142

intervention
    Intervention of the Competition Council before the Court of Appeals (Belgium) 87

investigation of infringement
    right of silence:
    Mannesmannröhren-Werke AG v Commission (EC) 65

investigation of state aid (*see* state aid)

Keyword Index

joint control (*see* control)

jurisdiction (*see also* block exemptions)
  de minimis *effect on national market:*
  Madrid Airport Cargo Operators (Spain)   127
  market share thresholds:
  De Minimis Notice (EC)   75
  De Beers/Rio Tinto/Ashton Mining; P&O/Antwerp Combined Terminals (Belgium)   85
  New Merger Notification Thresholds (The Netherlands)   125
  sub-national authorities:
  Draft Law Regarding Regional Competition Authorities (Spain)   134

legislative and policy developments
  Proposed Amendments to Competition Act (Denmark)   95
  Amendments to Competition Law (France)   103
  Electricity Sector Decision Body (Germany)   110
  Amendments to Competition Law (Italy)   122
  Change in Competition Authority Status (The Netherlands)   124
  Fining Guidelines (The Netherlands)   126
  Draft Regulation on Agreements Qualifying for EC Block Exemptions (Spain)   133
  Draft Law Regarding Regional Competition Authorities (Spain)   134
  Amendments to Competition Law (Spain)   135
  Decree on Merger Control Procedure (Spain)   135
  Group Exemption Regulations (Sweden)   140
  Proposed Amendments to Competition Act (Switzerland)   143
  Draft Act on Radio and Television (Switzerland)   144
  Life Insurance Market Recommendation (Switzerland)   144
  Interbrew (United Kingdom)   154
  Competition Regime Reforms (United Kingdom)   158
  Proposed Criminalization of "Hard Core" Cartel Activities (United Kingdom)   159
  Competition in Professions Report (United Kingdom)   160

leniency (*see* fines)

loyalty incentives (*see* fidelity incentives)

market definition
  Deutsche Post (EC)   16, 21
  Metsä Tissue/SCA Mölnlycke (EC)   29
  Tetra Pak/Sidel (EC)   34
  EDF/EnBW (EC)   36
  ADtranz/Bombardier (EC)   38
  MAN/Auwärter (EC)   41
  United Airlines/US Air (EC)   44
  Seagram/Pernod Ricard/Diageo (EC)   46

Keyword Index

    Smith & Nephew/Beiersdorf (EC)   49
    T-Online/TUI/C&N (EC)   50
    Højgaard & Schultz/Monberg & Thorsen (Denmark)   94
    Carlsberg/Coca-Cola Bottlers (Denmark)   94
    Pio Coronado/Cemetro (Spain)   131
    Nutreco España/Agrovic Alimentación (Spain)   131
    Scandinavian Airline System (Sweden)   138
    ICL (United Kingdom)   152
    Interbrew (United Kingdom)   154

market entry, barriers to (*see* barriers to market entry)

market share
    Draft Market Analysis Guidelines (EC)   23
    ADtranz/Bombadier (EC)   38
    MAN/Auwärter (EC)   41
    Degussa/Laporte (EC)   46
    De Minimis Notice (EC)   75
    BVBA Incine/NV Rendac (Belgium)   84
    New Merger Notification Thresholds (Belgium)   87
    Tryg Baltica (Denmark)   89
    Carlsberg (Denmark)   90
    AB/Provinzial (Denmark)   93
    Benetton (France)   99
    Sanacorp/Andrae-Noris Zahn (Germany)   108
    BP/Veba Oel; Shell/DEA (Germany)   109
    Communication on Vertical Agreements (Greece)   112
    Granarolo/Centrale del Latte di Vicenza (Italy)   120
    Enel/France Télécom/Infostrada (Italy)   121
    Iberdrola Redes (Spain)   132
    Scandinavian Airline System (Sweden)   138
    Svenska Girot/Bankgirocentralen BGC/Privatgiro/Postgirot (Sweden)   139
    Aberdeen Journals (United Kingdom)   151
    ICL (United Kingdom)   152

new hearing
    "New Hearing" Rule in Merger Proceedings (Belgium)   86

non-competition agreements
    Métropole Télévision, Suez-Lyonnaise des Eaux & others v Commission (EC)   68
    Real Estate Franchise Chain (Denmark)   90
    AB/Provinzial (Denmark)   93
    Communication on Vertical Agreements (Greece)112

notification
  failure to notify state aid:
  Ferring v Agence Centrale des Organismes de Sécurité Sociale (EC)   60
  failure to notify transaction:
  Hutchinson/RMPM/ECT (EC)   40
  Vinci/Groupe GTM (Belgium)   85
  Banque Nationale de Paris/Paribas (Switzerland)   143
  failure to object following notification:
  Unione Petrolifera (Italy)   116
  filing fees:
  Amendments to Competition Law (Spain)   135
  requirements, generally:
  Amendments to Competition Law (France)   103
  Decree on Merger Control Procedure (Spain)   135
  Foreign Concentrations (Switzerland)   144
  thresholds:
  New Merger Notification Thresholds (Belgium)   87
  New Merger Notification Thresholds (Italy)   123
  Competition Authority 2000 Annual Report (The Netherlands)   125
  New Merger Notification Thresholds (The Netherlands)   125
  Decree on Merger Control Procedure (Spain)   135

oligopoly (*see* collective dominance)

predatory pricing (*see* excessive pricing)

price discrimination (*see* discriminatory/differential pricing)

price fixing (*see* horizontal agreements)

price leadership doctrine
  Dairy Cartel (Spain)   128

price undercutting
  France Télécom (France)   68
  Napp Pharmaceuticals (United Kingdom)   147
  Aberdeen Journals (United Kingdom)   151

public exchange offer
  Schneider Electric/Legrand (EC)   33

public service obligation
  Ferring v Agence Centrale des Organismes de Sécurité Sociale (EC)   60

quotas
  GlaxoWellcome (Greece)   113

referral
>
from Commission to national authorities:
BP/Veba Oel; Shell/DEA (Germany)   109
Govia/Connex (United Kingdom)   157
Cargill/Cerestar (United Kingdom)   158
Interbrew (United Kingdom)   154
from national authorities to Commission:
Promatech/Sulzer (Germany, Italy, Spain, United Kingdom)   109, 122, 132, 158

refusal to supply goods or services
IMS Health (EC)   20
Deutsche Post (II) (EC)   21
Dansk Kørelærer Union (Denmark)   91
GlaxoWellcome (Greece)   113
Otis/Ceam/Kone/Schindler (Italy)   115
Telecom Italia (Italy)   117
General Insurance Standards Council (United Kingdom)   150
ICL (United Kingdom)   152

remand, effect of on waiting period
Linde-Verlag/Wolters Kluwer (Austria)   81

remedies (*see also* interim measures, fines, undertakings)
generally:
Courage v Crehan (EC)   3
Scandinavian Airline System (Sweden)   138
Teleclub (Switzerland)   142
Napp Pharmaceuticals (United Kingdom)   147
Yellow Pages (United Kingdom)   149
British Sky Broadcasting Limited (United Kingdom)   149
Mobile Phone Sector Inquiry (United Kingdom)   149
for completed mergers in merger control proceedings:
Schneider Electric/Legrand (EC)   33
Interbrew (United Kingdom)   154

resale restrictions
Ruko (Denmark)   92
Benetton (France)   99
GlaxoWellcome (Greece)   113
Termination of Medications Retail Price Maintenance Exemption (United Kingdom)   146

retaliatory potential
EDF/EnBW (EC)   36
Granarolo/Centrale del Latte di Vicenza (Italy)   120

rule of reason theory
  Métropole Télévision, Suez-Lyonnaise des Eaux & others v Commission (EC)   68

services of general economic interest
  TNT Traco v Poste Italiene (EC)   11
  Amendments to Competition Law (Italy)   122

special rights (*see* exclusive rights)

standing
  Callahan Associates/NetCologne (Germany)   106
  Lekkerland/Tobaccoland (Germany)   106

state aid (*see also* state resources; discriminatory taxation)
  effect of on trade between Member States:
  Regione Autonome Fruili-Venezia Giulia v Commission (EC)   63
  examination of in merger control proceedings:
  RJB Mining v Commission (EC)   62
  existing aid:
  Regione Autonome Fruili-Venezia Giulia v Commission (EC)   63
  failure to initiate within required time period:
  Austria v Commission (EC)   55
  when formal investigation required:
  Portuguese Republic v Commission (EC)   58

state resources
  PreussenElektra v Schlesswag (EC)   56
  Adria-Wien Pipeline v Finanzlandesdirektion für Kärnten (EC)   58
  Ferring v Agence Centrale des Organismes de Sécurité Sociale (EC)   60

substitute goods or services
  Tetra Pak/Sidel (EC)   34
  United Airlines/US Air (EC)   44
  T-Online/TUI/C&N (EC)   50

supervision of legal monopolies
  La Poste France (EC)   22

tax exemptions and rebates (*see* discriminatory taxation)

trademarks (*see* intellectual property)

turnover (*see* jurisdictional thresholds; notification thresholds)

undertakings
  generally:
  Notice on remedies (EC)   26

Keyword Index

  submission after deadline:
  Schneider Electric/Legrand (EC) 33
  divestitures:
  Metsä Tissue/SCA Mölnlycke (EC) 29
  General Electric/Honeywell (EC) 31
  EDF/EnBW (EC) 36
  ADtranz/Bombadier (EC) 38
  Degussa/Laporte (EC) 46
  Seagram/Pernod Ricard/Diageo (EC) 46
  Nestlé/Ralston Purina (EC) 47
  Smith & Nephew/Beiersdorf (EC) 49
  The Post Office/TNT/Singapore Post (EC) 49
  Kirch Group/EM.TV (Germany) 105
  VEBA/VIAG; RWE/VEW (Germany) 107
  BP/Veba Oel; Shell/DEA (Germany) 109
  Enel/France Télécom/Infostrada (Italy) 121
  Endesa/Iberdrola (Spain) 130
  Pio Coronado/Cemetro (Spain) 131
  Interbrew (United Kingdom) 154
  non-structural remedies:
  General Electric/Honeywell (EC) 31
  EDF/EnBW (EC) 36
  ADtranz/Bombadier (EC) 38
  Hidroelectrica del Cantabrico/Villar Mir/EnBW (EC) 39
  United Airlines/US Air (EC) 44
  Seagram/Pernod Ricard/Diageo (EC) 46
  Format/profil (Austria) 80
  DONG/Naturgas Sjælland Denmark) 92
  Boeing/Jeppsen Group (France) 102
  Deutsche Lufthansa/Eurowings (Germany) 107
  BP/Veba Oel; Shell/DEA (Germany) 109
  Seat Pagine Gialle/Cecchi Gori Communications (Italy) 119
  Endesa/Iberdrola (Spain) 130
  Nutreco España/Agrovic Alimentación (Spain) 131
  British Sky Broadcasting Limited (United Kingdom) 149

United States antitrust law and proceedings
  General Electric/Honeywell (EC) 31
  BASF/Eurodiol/Pantochim (EC) 42
  Métropole Télévision, Suez-Lyonnaise des Eaux & others v Commission (EC) 68
  Amino Acids (EC) 72
  Draft Leniency Notice (EC) 73
  Granarolo/Centrale del Latte di Vicenza (Italy) 120

Keyword Index

    Decree on Merger Control Procedure (Spain)   135
    Competition Regime Reforms (United Kingdom)   158

unjust enrichment
    Courage v Crehan (EC)   3

up-front buyer
    Notice on remedies (EC)   26
    The Post Office/TNT/Singapore Post (EC)   49
    Interbrew (United Kingdom)   154

vertical integration
    General Electric/Honeywell (EC)   31
    ADtranz/Bombadier (EC)   38
    Iberdrola Redes (Spain)   132

vertical restraints
    Courage v Crehan (EC)   3
    GlaxoWellcome Dual Pricing System (EC)   5
    Michelin (EC)   6
    Tryg Baltica (Denmark)   89
    Den Almindelige Danske Lægeforening (Denmark)   89
    Carlsberg (Denmark)   90
    Danish Football Association (Denmark)   90
    Real Estate Franchise Chain (Denmark)   90
    Canal+ (France)   97
    Benetton (France)   99
    Communication on Vertical Agreements (Greece)   112
    La Casera (Spain)   127
    Termination of Medications Retail Price Maintenance Exemption (United Kingdom)   146

volume discounts (*see* discriminatory/differential pricing or conditions)

For further information, please contact Romano Subiotto, Robbert Snelders or Kerri Vermeylen in the Brussels Office of Cleary, Gottlieb, Steen & Hamilton. BruECreports@cgsh.com

The information and views contained in this report are not intended to be a comprehensive study, nor to provide legal advice, and should not be treated as a substitute for specific advice concerning individual situations.